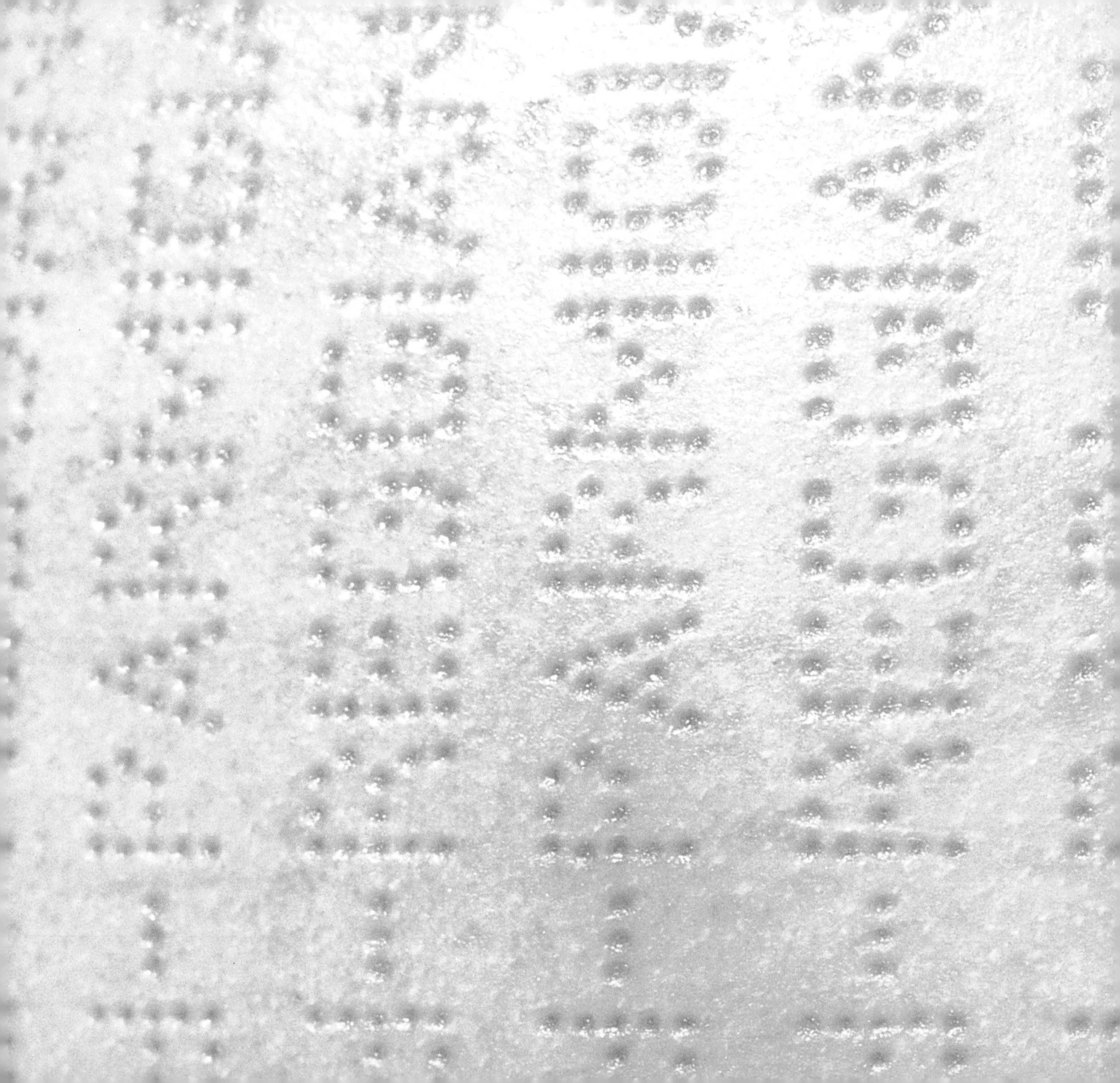

Parmigiano!

Parmigiano!

50 New & Classic Recipes with Parmigiano-Reggiano Cheese

Text and Recipes by Pamela Sheldon Johns

Produced by Jennifer Barry Design

Photography by Steven Rothfeld

Ten Speed Press
Berkeley, California

A Kirsty Melville Book

Ten Speed Press
Box 7123, Berkeley, California 94707

Distributed in Australia by E.J. Dwyer Pty. Ltd., in Canada by
Publishers Group West, in New Zealand by Tandem Press, in South Africa by
Real Books, and in the United Kingdom and Europe by Airlift Books.

Concept and Design: Jennifer Barry Design, Sausalito, California
Design and Production Assistant: Kristen Wurz
Copy Editor: Carolyn Miller
Food Stylist: Pouké
Food Stylist Assistant: Michelle Syracuse
Prop Stylist: Carol Hacker/Tableprop
Backgrounds: Michelle Syracuse, San Francisco

Library of Congress Cataloging-in-Publication Data
Johns, Pamela Sheldon, 1953–
Parmigiano! : 50 new & classic recipes with
parmigiano-reggiano cheese / Pamela Sheldon Johns.
        p.   cm.
Includes index.
ISBN 0-89815-937-7 (cloth)
1. Cookery (Cheese) 2. Cheese.
3. Parmigiano Reggiano cheese--History. I. Title.
Tx759.5.c48j66   1997
641.6'7358--dc21

Printed in China

First printing, 1997

1 2 3 4 5 6 7 8 9 10 — 00 01 99 98 97

CONTENTS

INTRODUCTION

"The origins of Parmigiano-Reggiano are certainly much earlier than the twelfth- and thirteenth-century literary sources which inform us of the existence and renown of this cheese. The area of origin is still the same as back then, with its borders marked by rivers and mountains; the rites of manufacturing are unchanged and the quality of production constant. The reason for such a lasting fidelity to a product cannot be only economic or alimentary. The history of Parmigiano-Reggiano is steeped in passion handed down from generation to generation…"

This quote by the past chairman of the Parmigiano-Reggiano Consortium, Giampaolo Mora, illustrates the depth of history of one of the world's greatest cheeses. Ask any Italian about Parmigiano-Reggiano, and with no shortage of passion, the king of Italian cheeses will be described in lengthy and loving terms. Those who make it refer to it as a living, breathing substance. As it ripens and refines with age, it evokes the drama of a region with a history filled with the contributions of artists, composers, singers, and nobility, and a landscape of green, green rolling pastures. In the north of Italy lies Emilia-Romagna, the heartland, the greatest source of agriculture in the country. It is the birthplace of many prized food products. Parmigiano-Reggiano, *aceto balsamico* (balsamic vinegar), and *prosciutto di Parma* are some of the most well known.

The story of Parmigiano-Reggiano is intricate, from the traditional details of the process of cheesemaking to the way it is marketed in today's world. It is analogous to a prehistoric stone-wheeled cart standing next to a superhighway. How will it manage to travel next to all of the fast-paced inventions of modern times?

Italy is undergoing a transformation, as is the rest of the developed world. It's hard to ignore technology, especially when it saves us time and money. Yet, in Italy, there is still a respect for tradition and a longing to maintain the flavors of the past. There is even a movement dedicated to fighting the growth of fast food. Called Slow Food, they proclaim themselves, "Dedicated to the defense of and the right to pleasure." In Italy, laws are written

Consortium Controlled Italian Cheeses

Many areas of Italy produce artisanal cheeses that are protected according to a law passed in 1955. This denomination of origin (D.O.C.), and legislature to protect the quality of other cheeses, serves to standarize the production methods and style of certain cheeses. Here are a few of the most widely known quality-protected cheeses:

Asiago

Caciocavallo

Fiore Sardo

Fontina

Gorgonzola

Grana Padano

Montasio

Mozzarella di Bufala

Parmigiano-Reggiano

Pecorino Romano

Pecorino Siciliano

Provolone

Robiola di Roccaverano

Taleggio

to protect its food artisans and their traditions. Self-regulating organizations, or consortiums, are formed to protect the standards and heritage of special foods. Parmigiano-Reggiano is one of those protected products.

The cows of Emilia-Romagna, locally known for their "river of milk," are fed specially formulated and restricted diets. Thanks to modern methods of animal husbandry, they produce milk 365 days a year. Therefore, every day of the year, the cheese-maker is at work, starting at the crack of dawn.

Parmigiano-Reggiano is simply a combination of milk, rennet, salt, and time. What is it, then, that makes it so unique? And what are the best uses for such a precious commodity? Understanding the history, the territory, and the manufacturing process of the cheese provides insight into the special position Parmigiano-Reggiano holds throughout the world. The recipes in this book provide good examples of the many wonderful ways it can enhance your cooking. The throne for the king of Italian cheeses, however, is on the table. As a table cheese, grated fresh over piping hot food, or simply wedged off in jagged shards to nibble on, Parmigiano-Reggiano rules!

What Is Grana?

Parmigiano-Reggiano belongs to a category of cheeses called *grana,* hard, aged cheeses with an internal structure that is granular in appearance and texture. The word literally means grain, but in Italian slang it can also mean trouble or money.

After Parmigiano-Reggiano, Grana Padano is the best known of Italian *grana* cheeses. There has been throughout history, and continues to be, ample competition in the distinction between these two similar products. Grana Padano is made in areas adjacent to the geographic zone determined for Parmigiano-Reggiano. The *zona tipica*, or region of origin, for Grana Padano is specifically designated and controlled by law in the same way as that for Parmigiano-Reggiano. This area covers the Po River Valley which reaches across the whole north of Italy throughout the provinces of Lombardy, Emilia-Romagna, the Veneto, and Trentino. Some *grane* are named after a region, such as Lodi's Grana Lodigiano, whose history is as long as that of Parmigiano-Reggiano.

Some of the best Grana Padano can rival lesser Parmigiano-Reggiano. They are essentially the same shape and size. The process for making Grana Padano is similar and is also controlled, but the

Grana

In Treasures of the Italian Table, *Burton Anderson relates a visit to Parmigiano-Reggiano producer Peppino Mornini's small* casello *in the hills south of Reggio. When asked to tell about his career, Peppino chuckled, "My career? Well, what else would a* casaro *do but make* grana?" *He laughed with what turned out to be his customary exuberance as* Casali *[Anderson's guide] explained the pun;* grana, *besides cheese, is slang for dough or scratch (as in money), as well as for trouble or scandal.*

Peppino came back: "But in my case it just means formaggio."

restrictions are less stringent than for Parmigiano-Reggiano. For example, the defined technique for making Grana Padano allows adding saffron for color and will permit the use of anti-fermentatives in the cows' diets, methods that are not permitted in the production of Parmigiano-Reggiano. You can recognize Grana Padano by its firebrand, a diamond-like trademark burned into the side of the cheese. It is a guarantee that the minimum standard of quality outlined by law is present. While the variations in *grana* are greater due to its expansive geography, the prices are consistently lower, which has made it a competitive product to Parmigiano-Reggiano.

In Italy, there are other regions producing good *grana*, sometimes from sheep's or goat's milk. But each step away from the locus of quality identified by Parmigiano-Reggiano leads to lesser versions. Other countries produce *grana*, but none of them can rival the cheeses of northern Italy. Pricing is a consideration; Reggianito, from Argentina and Uruguay, for example, is half the price. American producers, including one who emigrated to the United States from Parma, are also trying to create a viable competitor. The best advice, aside from buying Parmigiano-Reggiano, is to taste any *grana* before purchasing, if possible.

History

The origin of cheese is certainly ancient, a food born of necessity. As far back as the eleventh century Benedictine monks had developed methods for long preservation of cheese for their legendary pilgrimages from abbey to abbey. The Roman foot soldiers carried only a little grain, aged cheese, and wine on their country-long treks. Somewhere, someone, either out of hunger or curiosity, must have tried a taste of a milk that had curdled. Some historians believe that the first taste may have come from the stomach of a slaughtered calf, where the natural rennet in the calf's stomach had curdled the milk it drank. Or, a container of milk may have come in contact with wild artichokes, for this vegetable contains the rennet used to make one of the earliest cheeses, the Etruscan Marzolino.

The practice of brining and aging hard cheese has been well documented; some sources prove the existence of a *grana* cheese identified with Parma by name. One of the most quoted is a fanciful story worth repeating:

The Renaissance writer Giovanni Boccaccio is famous for his book of tales, *The Decameron (Decamerone)*, which literally translates to "ten days' work." The story of a group of young Florentines who go to the countryside for ten days to escape the bubonic plague in Florence, it is filled with the one hundred tales they told to entertain themselves during the wait. In the third story of the eighth day, the character Maso tells a story of an imaginary paradise, the land of Bengodi. In this paradise was a mountain of grated Parmesan cheese, on top of which were people who did nothing but make macaroni and ravioli. When the pasta was rolled down to the bottom of the mountain, it was coated with the lovely cheese. Clearly, when this was written, in 1348 to 1353, Florentines were quite familiar with a hard grating cheese from Parma.

Early widespread international interest in Parmigiano was effected by trade. The cheese is mentioned in numerous publications in France as early as the sixteenth century. In the 1780 *Encyclopédie* by Diderot and d'Alembert, Parmesan is defined as "... the name given to a hard cheese that is highly valued by the Italians and produced in the Parma region, from whence it is exported to all of Europe." Its scope reached beyond Europe, often as gifts to foreign heads of state. Even Thomas Jefferson had it imported to the new union of states in America. Export records from Reggio Emilia in 1913, show that of the 7,400 tons of cheese produced, approximately 3,000 tons were exported.

Zona Tipica

The *zona tipica* is the legally identified area in which certain cheeses can be produced. This delineation can be compared to winemaking D.O.C. zones, or the *Denominazione di Origine Controllata* (denomination of controlled origin), which not only controls the geographic origin of specific wines, but also outlines permitted ingredients and defines the production and aging process. The *zona tipica* for Parmigiano-Reggiano is in the region of Emilia-Romagna, bounded by rivers and mountains, as it was in ancient times. The heart of the zone is the Enza Valley, where the first *grana* cheese was perhaps made. The Enza River divides the provinces of Parma and Reggio nell'Emilia (also known simply as Reggio), and historically there was major competition between the two.

Although historians believe that Parmigiano originated in the Enza Valley of Reggio, most historical references call the cheese Parmigiano. That word can refer to a person, a dish, a cheese, or an item from Parma. *Alla parmigiano* is a culinary term, for a dish that has been sprinkled with Parmigiano and gratinéed. Understanding the history helps explain how the cheese acquired its name: Reggio Emilia was once part of the Duchy of Parma. The amount of trade and foreign visitors passing through Parma gave strength to the association between the cheese and that city. In recent times, when legislation standardized the production of Parmigiano cheese, a modern-day compromise was reached by titling the cheese with both provincial names. In the war of cheeses, both sides of the valley now have equal status, but many think the best Parmigiano-Reggiano comes from the area near the Enza River on the Reggio side. In addition to the provinces of Parma and Reggio Emilia, the boundaries of the *zona tipica* extend to include Modena, Mantua on the right bank of the Po River, and Bologna on the left bank of the Reno River.

The countryside here is dotted with ancient *caselli,* octagonal cheesemaking buildings of brick with lattice windows for light and ventilation. The beauty of this area is an austere one, especially in winter when the plains are below freezing and foggy. But in the spring, the land becomes a sweeping sea of green. By early summer you see scarlet poppies, and soon, miles and miles of sunflowers. Even in the autumn, the colors are lush and inviting. Surprisingly, cows are rarely seen in this pastoral landscape. The rich land is an agricultural wonder, and the affluence afforded by the fine commodities it produces has made the land too precious to let cows and pigs graze and roam, trampling the grasses.

Emilia-Romagna is referred to as the heartland of Italy. Once completely under water, the swamps were drained in the thirteenth and fourteenth centuries. Irrigation was utilized, resulting in fertile land that continues to produce many fruits, grains, wines, and oil, as well as the nutritious fodder for the cows that makes the milk for Parmigiano-Reggiano, known as the richest milk in Italy.

Is it any surprise, then, that the country's largest dairies, grain-based industries, and produce-preserving plants are here? Agriculture has become a giant, and along with it, concern has grown over environmental problems due to the use of commercial fertilizers and pesticides, and depletion of the natural minerals and richness of the land from overuse.

The production of Parmigiano-Reggiano has boomed, as well, and the industry is now imposing quotas to ensure quality controls. It has the feel of a big business, with more cooperatives and fewer small farms. Competition is difficult for the smaller producers, due to the demand by cooperatives for the milk. Often a price war flares up between individual dairies and cooperatives. In spite of this, Parmigiano-Reggiano is still a handmade product, and for that reason, the small producers with good cheese can continue to survive. As the consortium for protection of the cheese states, "For seven hundred years and more we have paid the price of toil, obedience and experience for the right to live by creating something that kings and commoners proclaim good. Nothing but milk, rennet, and fire ever went into the making of cheese."

The people of Emilia-Romagna have a reputation for hard work. They take joy in their labor and celebrate in the rewards. Their passion for art and music and their gusto for perfection in food come together to create an environment for excellence. In a region known for composers, opera stars, and artists such as Giuseppi Verdi, Luciano Pavarotti, Arturo Toscanini, and Fellini, to speak of passion is an understatement. Centuries of abundance have also resulted in a legendary heritage of many gastronomic classics: Parmigiano-Reggiano, of course, but also *prosciutto di Parma, aceto balsamico* (balsamic vinegar), and several classic pasta dishes such as *tortellini in brodo*. The hearty food reflects the agricultural history and the dietary needs of the region's working farmers. Yet it is also a refined cuisine, complex and labor-intensive, that begins with the product and culminates on the plate.

There are no holidays for the cheese-maker. Since the advent of artificial insemination, the dairyman has cows lactating year-round. So, when the Consorzio del Formaggio Parmigiano-Reggiano offered to take me for a visit to see the cheese being made, I knew that as far as the cows were concerned I had my choice of days. But I didn't have my choice of hours, for the process begins early in the morning.

I rose with the sun, for the hour-long drive to Parma from my *agriturismo,* a farmhouse inn, in Castelfranco Emilia, near Modena. This was no easy task, considering the sumptuous farmhouse dinner and local wines I had enjoyed the night before. I drove the Via Emilia, a road made in 187 B.C. to connect ancient Rome to its distant colonies, knowing that if it grew late I could hop onto the autostrada that parallels it.

After meeting my host from the consortium, Alfredo Busani, in Parma, we drove south to the village of Marano. I thought I was up early, but the morning's milk had already been delivered, and the Campanini family was busily at work. This particular *casello* belongs to a cooperative of milk producers who pay the salary of cheese-maker

**Making
Parmigiano-Reggiano:
A Time-Honored Process**

*The evening's
collection of milk is left
to rest overnight.
In the morning,
the milk is partially
skimmed and added to
the fresh whole milk.
Natural whey ferments
are added.
The mixture is heated
until it curdles.
The curdles are broken
into tiny granules.
The curd is cooked
and drained.
The cheese is placed
in forms.
Stencils are put in
place to mark the date
and dairy .
When firm, the cheese
is placed in brine baths
for 20 to 30 days.
The cheese is drained
and placed in vaults to
age for 12 to 24 months.*

15

Campanini. The Latteria Cooperativa di Marano, No. 2471, is a relatively new cooperative. While it has only been registered for two years, Signore Campanini has been making cheese most of his life. The *casaro*, or dairyman, works a ten- to fifteen-year apprenticeship with a master cheese-maker. Campanini's son Massimo works closely with him now, learning the trade from his father, and will one day take over the position of cheese-maker.

The expansive work-room was a surprise for me, as all of the producers I had ever visited were small farm operations. Here was a gleaming laboratory in every sense of the word, with white tile, chrome fixtures and work tables, and great copper cauldrons. Milk  from the previous night's milking had been placed in wide, oversized stainless steel trays overnight to allow the cream to separate and the milk to begin its fermentation. In the morning before we arrived, part of the cream had been removed to be used for butter. Here is where the cheese-maker's skill is vital: The amount of cream skimmed must be directly proportionate to the amount of casein, or protein, in the milk. The ideal is to leave as much

fat as possible in the milk, but the protein content will only support so much. The greater the fat, the longer a cheese can age, creating a more complex cheese. This protein level varies at different times of the year, so when it is higher, usually in the early fall, less cream may be skimmed, resulting in a cheese that has a slightly higher fat level and is just a little richer. Accurate records are kept for the origin of each batch of milk. In the event of a problem with the cheese, it can be traced back to the dairy that provided the milk.

At this stage of the cheesemaking process, Campanini, working with his son and daughter-in-law, blends the partially skimmed milk with fresh whole milk that has just arrived. This is poured into the huge bell-shaped copper vats. The copper is an important element, not only because it is the ultimate heat-conducting material, but also because it causes an acidic reaction with the milk. As it begins to heat, Campanini adds the starter, a portion of the whey from the previous day's cheese-making that has fermented overnight to develop the lactic flora needed to raise the acid content. Testing to ensure that the acid balance is correct is critical to the end product. The mixture is now heated and supplemented with rennet to induce curdling. Rennet is the only non-milk additive that is allowed. Part of the traditional process, it is obtained from the stomachs of suckling calves.

This modern dairy has electronically controlled stirring devices and thermometers, thank goodness, as they have twelve copper vats working at the same time! Each vat holds 245 gallons of milk and will yield two forms of cheese. Now, the cheesemakers are moving constantly in an economy of motion. As the mixture cooks, it begins to form soft curds and separates into solids and whey within fifteen minutes. Campinini strains out pieces from time

to time, squeezing them between his fingers to feel for the right consistency. Then, at just the right moment he employs the *spino*, a large stainless steel tool that looks like a giant egg whisk. *Spino* translates to "thornbush," the ancient tool which was once used for the task of breaking the curdled mass into tiny curds the size of rice. No machine has been developed for this. Campinini stirs and agitates the curds with great vigor. Finally, he is

satisfied that the curds are evenly riced, the mixture is heated again for another 12 to 15 minutes, watched very carefully until it is at a precise temperature of 55°C (131°F), and the curds have firmed. This is seldom a routine process. There are daily differences in behavior of the milk, and the cheesemaker is trained to respond to the visual and tactile cues presented.

The mixture is left to rest and cool slightly for half an hour. As it does, the gleaming mass comes together into a large ball at the bottom of the cauldron. Campanini and his son work together in a carefully choreographed maneuver to bring it to the surface and capture it in a piece of handwoven cheesecloth made of hemp and linen. Tied to a large dowel, it hangs over the pot to drain. This is hard work, for each mass probably weighs 150 pounds. At this stage the cheese looks like a glistening white ball of yeasty dough. Campinini now makes the rounds again, cutting each lump in half and kneading them into two separate rounds. Each half is placed in a plastic circular mold lined with cheesecloth, then set on a long wooden table. A heavy wooden disk is

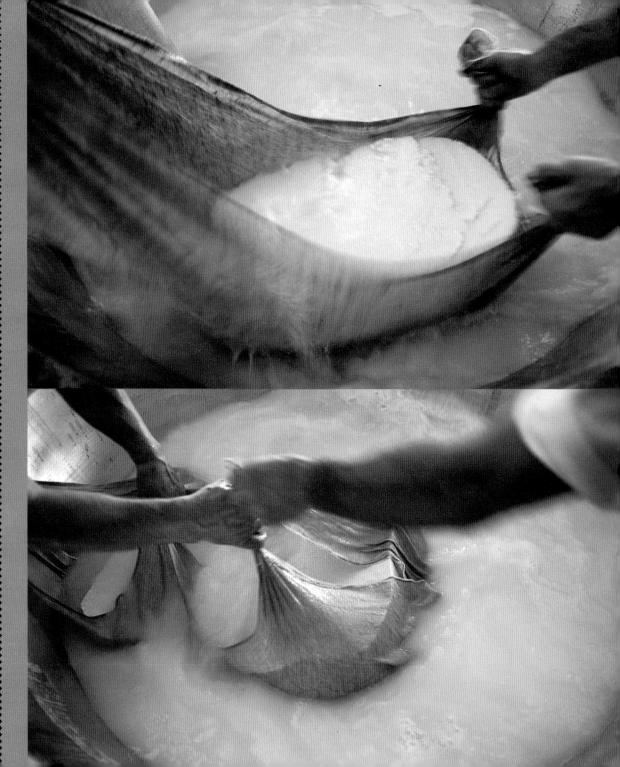

The Birth of the Cheese

*Top left: After resting
for half an hour, the curd
comes together in a large
ball at the bottom of the
cauldron. It is then lifted
with a wooden paddle
and caught in a piece
of handwoven cheesecloth
made of hemp and linen.*

*Top right: The ball
is cut in half to create
two cheeses.*

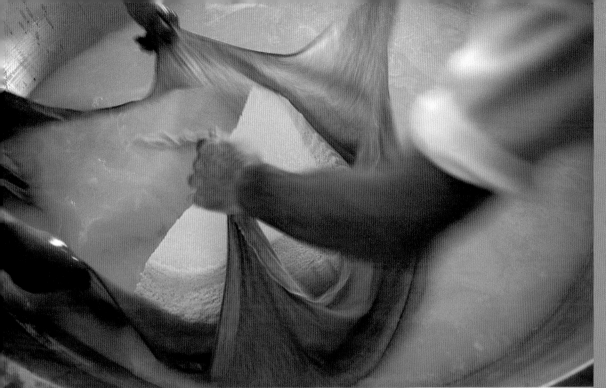

Bottom left: Now that there are two cheeses, a second piece of cloth is introduced to hold the other half.

Bottom right: The cheese-maker and his helper work together to maneuver the "babies" into position and tie them to a large dowel, where they will drain, suspended over the vat.

placed on top to gently force out some of the moisture and to keep the cheese from cooling too quickly. As it drains, the cheese is turned and the cloth is changed every two hours. The cheese begins to firm up, and within a few hours, the mold is temporarily removed to insert the Parmigiano-Reggiano stencil. This is a matrix of dots in a plastic band that will spell out the name PARMIGIANO-REGGIANO in upper-case letters around the entire rim of the cheese. Also included in the impression is the month, year, and number of the dairy. The mold is then replaced and the cheese continues to drain for a few days, being turned from top to bottom periodically so that both sides will be flattened.

The liquid left in the cauldron after draining the curd is the whey. Some will be set aside in a covered container to ferment for tomorrow's starter, and the rest be used either to make ricotta, or to feed the pigs. No wonder *prosciutto di Parma* is so sweet!

After two to three days of drying, the cheese will hold its shape and the mold is removed. We left that morning's cheeses in their molds to visit the brining and aging rooms. What a contrast to the light and airy laboratory. The brining room was cool, dark, and eerie, with the cheeses bobbing lightly in their salted water. They remain in brine for 20 to 25 days, and are turned daily to ensure that the salt is evenly distributed. After one more short draining session, the cheese is placed on wooden shelves to age for a minimum of twelve months before it is inspected and released to finish aging with a distributor for a minimum of six more months. While aging, it is often kept in cheese banks vaults with high security, for it is a precious commodity. Some banks hold as many as 200,000 cheeses, which can be used as collateral for loans. There have even been cheese-bank robberies, although since all of the cheeses are dated and numbered, they must be fairly easy to trace.

We entered the aging vault with a sense of reverence. Shelves from the very high ceiling to the floor were stacked with thousands of cheeses in different stages of readiness. The room was filled with a dense aroma, yet it was airy. It was our good luck to have inspector Busani, from the consortium with us. Campanini carefully selected one of the wheels of cheese and placed it on a small round wooden table obviously made just for that purpose. Busani explained that as the

**The Art of
Parmigiano-Reggiano**

*Leo Bertozzi,
vice president of marketing
for the Consorzio del
Formaggio Parmigiano-
Reggiano describes the
cheese as, "30 percent milk,
70 percent artisan."
More than milk,
rennet, and salt, it is
history, culture, agriculture,
economics, and even
technology are all
packaged in each
36-kilogram wheel.*

cheese ages and dries, it is turned, dusted, and visually inspected for oiliness or off-coloring. Bacteria growth can cause holes to form, creating hollow sounds that can be detected by the tapping of the inspector's hammer. He showed us the instruments he uses to inspect each wheel of cheese before it is branded. In addition to the *martello*, the hammer for sounding holes, the inspector uses an *ago*, a needlelike auger that is screwed into the cheese. This tool is used to check the fragrance of the cheese. The inspector can also tell what the interior is like by the degree of resistance as the *ago* is screwed in. The *sonda* is a probe that looks like half an apple corer; it removes a sample of the cheese when necessary.

Cheeses found to have problems, or that even appear suspicious, are scored with giant X's all around the rim to obscure the Parmigiano-Reggiano stencil. Called *grana da pasto*, table cheese, it is sold as an inferior cheese at a discount to locals; it is never exported. Only a perfect cheese will make it to the point that it receives the firebrand, a seal of the consortium, the final validation.

The people in the room with us were speaking in hushed tones as Busani worked away on this round of cheese, tapping and probing. I was surprised to see him scoring the rind of the cheese in a line that neatly marked it in half until I realized that he was about to open a cheese for us. My voice became hushed as well.

Once he had scored a shallow line all the way around, he wedged in two knives with short almond-shaped blades. On top, at each end of the diameter line, the knives were inserted and gently wedged to begin to open the cheese. Busani nudged and drove the knives deeper, until in a breathtaking flash, the cheese fell open, perfectly in half. Ah, the aroma! Tawny yellow flakes of the cheese found their way rather quickly into my mouth, where I felt the sizzle of the amino acids dancing on my tongue. Campinini was smiling and nodding.

The Cows

Today's "milk machines" are the approximately 200,000 *Frisona Italiana* cows, specially bred descendents of North American Holsteins and Dutch Fresians. In 1693, a Swiss friar, Georg König, described the cows that produced the "famous Parmesan cheese" as large, not tall, with red and black patches. These were probably the *Razza Reggiana* or *Vacche Rosse*, the red cows bred in Reggio since the Middle Ages. Over time they were phased out because they had a very low yield. They were replaced by the Swiss Bruna-Alpina, which turned out to be too delicate, a cow more suited to the mountains. Both breeds had low yields of milk, but their milk had a good protein content, which is important for making a rich cheese. Most of these cows were lost in World War II and were replaced with Holsteins from Poland, then improved in 1970 with the North American variety.

The Frisona is a big producer, averaging twenty-five liters a day, hence the name "milk machine," but the protein content of its milk is lower than that of the older breeds, which means the cheese cannot age as long. The Vacche Rosse are making a small comeback at a handful of dairies. Because they cannot produce as many cheeses, Parmigiano-Reggiano made from their milk is more expensive. Look for a logo with two red cows pulling a cart.

With the exception of very rural locales, the cows are not allowed to forage. They live in restricted areas with no free grazing. Their food, often computer-monitored, is brought to them. It contains grasses, alfalfa, and some cereal and will differ somewhat with the region. The sub-Alpine areas have more fresh grasses and clovers. On the plains and in the valleys, food is imported and often dried. Since no anti-fermentation additives are allowed, to be safe, some farmers prefer to use dry food when fresh is not readily available. All milk from all dairies is not uniform, and is not expected to be. These variations contribute to the uniqueness of the end product.

The Consorzio del Formaggio Parmigiano-Reggiano

Throughout the history of cheesemaking, the business relationship between the dairymen providing the milk and the cheese-maker has been an uneasy one. Poor milk can jeopardize a cheese-maker dependent on its quality, and an inadequately produced cheese can do the same to the dairyman.

As the popularity of Parmigiano-Reggiano grew, milk producers needed to find ways to maintain quality and become better organized to handle the greater demand. In small regional areas, the farmers became highly competitive. The sometimes bitter and jealous rivalry drove some dairies out of business in the nineteenth century. Eventually, it became apparent to the farmer that they needed to work together to promote the product and protect its individuality. After World War I, cooperatives were formed. This led to increased commercial success, but soon there were problems with controls and the introduction of technology. It was clear that a neutral body was needed to mediate the situation. The Consortium for the Protection of Parmigiano-Reggiano was founded in 1934, in Reggio Emilia. The goal was to offer the region a tool to effect harmony between progress and tradition, while considering social, political, economic, gastronomic, and cultural factors.

In 1951, nine European countries met to form an international agreement to formalize the definition and qualifications of twenty-three typical cheeses, including Parmigiano-Reggiano. The definition and amendments that followed two and four years later prescribed the limits of the production area, which was the same area designated in 1934 by the consortium.

Regulations changed in 1984. Up until this time, Parmigiano-Reggiano was allowed to be produced only between April 1 and November 11, when the cows were lactating. With the advent of year-round lactation, the laws governing the production of Parmigiano-Reggiano were adjusted to allow the cheese to be made during every month of the year.

Today, the consortium, a nonprofit agency, is supported by contributions from the 650 cheese producers. Each producer contributes 8,500 lire per cheese, about $5.50, for the services provided. It is a regulating body, but it also exists to protect the quality of the product. Its scientists test and monitor the milk quality and cows' food in over ten thousand dairies. They are responsible for the inspection and the official branding of cheeses, which is a guarantee that all regulated standards have been met. Besides the inspection and government of the regulations, the consortium fills an important promotional role. One of its goals is to facilitate trade and export; consequently, it establishes prices, quotas, and distribution policies. In 1996, approximately 2.9 million cheeses were produced. Of that, 7 percent was exported. The United States has import quotas as well. Laws in the 1950s established maximum importation quantities on cow's milk cheeses to protect U.S. dairies. Those quotas are still in effect for five Italian cheeses: Parmigiano-Reggiano, Grana Padano, Provolone, Provoletti, and cow's milk Romano.

The consortium registers each dairy and issues a specific number of the plastic bands used to stencil the trademark into the cheese. These plastic bands are highly monitored to prevent counterfeits.

The trademark that identifies authentic Parmigiano-Reggiano is a picture of a whole wheel of cheese resting on its rim with the words PARMIGIANO-REGGIANO repeated all around the circumference. Next to the wheel is a generous wedge of cheese resting on a plate with the traditional almond-shaped cheese knife. This picture is seen on labels of portioned cheeses and on roadside vendors' signage.

Consortium Standards for Parmigiano-Reggiano
According to a law passed in 1955, and amended in 1983 and 1990, the name Parmigiano-Reggiano can only be applied to cheese that meets the following rigorous requirements.

Zone of Production: The registered territory comprises the provinces of Bologna on the left bank of the Reno River and Mantua on the right bank of the Po River, and all of the provinces of Modena, Parma, and Reggio Emilia.

Process: This firm-textured cheese of medium butterfat content is prepared over heat and requires slow maturing. It is produced by coagulation with fermentation acids, and made from the milk of cows whose basic nourishment consists of heterogeneous fresh pasture grass. The yield of two successive milkings (evening and morning) is used after resting and partial skimming, without benefit of any artificial additives.

The curd is made with the aid of calves' rennet. The use of anti-fermentatives is not allowed. Within a few days, the cheese is salted, a process which takes approximately 20 to 30 days. Maturing is natural and must continue for at least 12 months, but the maturation process lasts much longer.

Description: The matured cheese is used plain or grated and presents the following features:
• A cylindrical shape with slightly convex to almost vertical sides, the flat ends being slightly bordered;
• Dimensions: diameter 35 to 45 cm, height 18 to 24 cm;
• External feature: oily dark color, or natural golden yellow;
• Color of internal mass: light to medium straw yellow;
• Characteristic flavor and aroma of the cheese: fragrant, delicate, savory, mild, but not piquant;
• Internal structure: minutely granulated, exhibiting internal scale-formation, minute holes barely visible to the eye;
• Thickness of rind: about 6 mm;
• Butterfat content on dry matter: 32 percent minimum.

The Cheese: Description, Marking, Nutrition

Parmigiano-Reggiano is a product of many influences, some manageable, some uncontrollable, including the environment, the milk itself, traditional techniques and modern advances, agricultural conditions, animal husbandry, dairy operations, and business and international trade policies.

Leo Bertozzi, vice president of marketing for the Consorzio del Formaggio Parmigiano-Reggiano, describes the cheese as, "30 percent milk, 70 percent artisan." History, culture, agriculture, economics, and even technology are all packaged in each 36-kilogram wheel.

In more tangible terms, Parmigiano-Reggiano can be described as follows:

Dimensions/Weight: An $8^1/2$- to $9^1/2$-inch-high cylinder, 16 to 18 inches in diameter, with an average weight of 70 to 80 pounds.

Color: From pale yellow or straw to tawny and amber, influenced by the cows' diet and the length of the aging of the cheese.

Texture: The name, *grana*, refers to its grainy texture. It is striated with tiny white crystals, which are amino acids, not salt. On close inspection you can see minute holes. As pieces are wedged from a chunk, the cheese flakes should fall off the cheese.

Taste: Full and sparkling, but not sharp; longer aging yields a more complex flavor and flaky texture.

Markings: Every cheese that has passed consortium inspection will have the following:
• The PARMIGIANO-REGGIANO stencil vertically repeated from top to bottom around the entire form, so that every piece of cheese cut from the wheel will have this marking on its rind.
• The dairy's registration number and the month/year of production is also stenciled on the rind. The month name abbreviations are similar to English, except for January's (GEN) and July's (LUG).
• After the twelve-month inspection, the inspector for the consortium burns on the stamp of approval, a firebrand oval with CONSORZIO TUTELA in the center, PARMIGIANO REGGIANO on the border. This is the guarantee that the cheese has met the criteria set forth by the consortium.

Additional seals appear on some cheeses:
• Cut and packaged cheeses must bear a label with the registered trademark, a stamp that looks like the firebrand, along with the symbolic picture of a whole form, a wedge, and the traditional cutting tool.
• Cheeses for export are branded with a special marking to certify quality and a minimum of eighteen months of aging. Whole wheels are firebranded, and when the cheese is portioned for export, the trademark for export will be on the label.

• Packaged grated cheese: Only five producers in Italy are allowed to package grated Parmigiano-Reggiano. The label bears the trademark, along with the word *GRATTUGIATO*, which means grated. These producers must make a monetary deposit that stands behind their guarantee that the cheese is 100 percent Parmigiano-Reggiano. It must have a minimum water content of 25 percent, and shelf life is limited to maintain quality assurance.
• Certain producers have a personal notation, such as Notari's Vacche Rosse brand with two red cows pulling a cart. Some cheeses are marked by selectors, specialists who pick a cheese by the dairy and/or season. Rocca is one such selector, known

for choosing exceptional cheese.
• If you see giant X's obscuring the Parmigiano-Reggiano stencil, this is *grana da pasto*, cheese that has been rejected by the inspector.

Price: The retail price in the United States averages from $12 to $15 per pound. A wheel costs nearly $1,000.

Nutrition: Compared to other cheeses, Parmigiano-Reggiano rates well for nutrition. It is lower in fat than most, at 28 to 32 percent. Italians consider Parmigiano-Reggiano a valuable source of energy, easily digested by babies and the elderly alike. It has lots of protein (33 percent) and is a good source of calcium. It is low in lactose, milk's natural sugar, which is difficult for some people to digest. The lactose is in the whey, of which 98 percent is removed when the cheese separates and is drained; the rest is metabolized in the fermentation process. It is important to know if you are looking at the nutritional numbers by weight or measure. The weight of grated cheese is considerably less for the same volume of solid cheese. One tablespoon of grated Parmigiano equals 28 calories, 3 grams of protein, and 2 grams of fat. One-half ounce of solid cheese, a comparable amount by weight, contains 55 calories, 5 grams of protein, and 3.5 grams of fat. Because this cheese has such an intense flavor, you need only a little for a great impact.

Opening the Cheese

Top left: The rind is scored shallowly all the way around creating a guideline to divide halves.

Top right: On top, at each end of the diameter line, knives with almond-shaped blades are inserted and gently wedged in to begin to open the cheese.

Bottom left: The knives are nudged and wedged in slowly.

Bottom right: The cheese breaks evenly in half, revealing the grainy interior. It is then cut into pie-shaped wedges so that every portion has a piece of the rind.

31

Buying Parmigiano-Reggiano

The cheese is at its prime the moment it is opened. Once it is exposed to the air, the flavor begins a gradual decline. You probably won't be buying a whole wheel, but if you do, plan on using it quickly once it is opened. If your supplier offers only portions, try to buy cheese that has been vacuum packed to avoid contact with the air. When buying chunks, as most of us do, shop at a supplier with a high turnover. Ask for a cheese that has been freshly opened. Take a good look at it; it should not have holes or appear dried out, rubbery, or oily, and it should flake when chipped. Try to buy pieces with rind, not just for identification, but also because the rind helps to keep the cheese from drying out too fast. Never buy the cheese grated. Grating exposes cheese to the air, which robs it of flavor rather quickly. Grate only as you need it.

The traditional way to open a whole cheese is to start by drawing a guideline to divide halves. The rind is scored shallowly all the way around with a notched knife called the *segna forme*. On top, at each end of the diameter line, two Parmigiano-Reggiano knives are inserted and wedged to open the cheese. It should break evenly in half, and from there, cut in pie shaped wedges so that every piece has a portion of the rind.

In the rare event that you are given a choice of cheeses, consider the dairy numbers. Often the lower numbers belong to older dairies, possibly from a rural area where the cows are fed more green fodder. This numbering system is not foolproof, for as the older dairies go out of business, the lower numbers are sometimes reassigned to new dairies, which are likely to be large, modern cooperatives. Ask which area the cheese is from, the mountains or the plains. Mountain cheeses from the fall season are often more robust due to the second growth of green grass available in the early fall.

Cheese from the same producer varies from season to season. So, given the option, consider the date. Spring cheeses must age over two summers, whereas a winter cheese has more cool weather in its eighteen-month aging. Spring cheese may be ready at an earlier age, while maintaining a lighter quality. The color may be more yellow from the carotene in yellow flowers found in spring fodder. Winter cheese can develop more slowly and age a little longer. While in the past, Parmigiano-Reggiano improved with lengthy aging, today, due to the lower protein content of the milk, two years is the optimum age suggested.

Storing Parmigiano-Reggiano

Once a cheese is open, it will retain its best flavor for 1 month if stored properly. To do so, wrap the cheese in parchment paper, then in plastic or aluminum foil and refrigerate. If the cheese begins to dry out, wrap it in a moist towel for a day in the refrigerator, then remove the towel and rewrap the cheese in parchment and plastic. Do not freeze Parmigiano-Reggiano.

Cooking with Parmigiano-Reggiano

Contessa Rosetta Clara Cavalli d'Olivola owns Principato di Lucedio in Piedmont, one of Italy's finest rice-growing estates. The Contessa is known both for her risotto, and also for the way she serves it: She cuts a Parmigiano-Reggiano wheel in half around the circumference, then scoops out most of the cheese from one of the halves. When her risotto is ready to serve, she pours it into the hollowed-out form. As it is served from the Parmigiano-Reggiano "bowl," bits of residual cheese are melted in and scraped out with the risotto.

For our everyday cooking, we may not go to such lengths. The most common preparation of Parmigiano-Reggiano is to grate it. Grating by hand yields a fluffier condiment, but for use in cooking, it is quickest to use the food processor. The processor's steel knife blade pulverizes the cheese to an even consistency. Cut it into small chunks. Do not try to process ice-cold cheese; let it sit at room temperature for a short time so that it is not so hard. Traditional cheese graters can be used to grate for coarse or fine grating. A vegetable peeler works well for shavings. Small chips and and larger shards should be made by wedging off chunks with a cheese knife.

All parts of the cheese are edible. The rind bolsters the flavors of soups and stews when simmered along with the rest of the ingredients. Parmigiano-Reggiano is famous as a gratin topping. It's also a great addition to breading mixtures and melts well into sauces. It goes with most foods, except perhaps very fishy or spicy dishes. In *Classic Techniques of Italian Cooking*, Giuliano Bugialli describes a popular eighteenth-century sorbet of Parmigiano. It is an unsweetened creamy iced dish that is served as a cheese course.

Serving Parmigiano-Reggiano

In its royal position as a table cheese, Parmigiano-Reggiano should be served in a large chunk at room temperature. Grate it at the table or wedge off bite-sized pieces as needed. The ideal implement for portioning out Parmigiano is an Italian cheese knife with a short blade shaped like an almond. It is thin-bladed on one side, and acts as a wedge to open the cheese, rather than cutting it. Slicing crushes the amino crystals; you will find that the cheese tastes better when it is allowed to fall off in jagged chunks.

Openers

BABY ARTICHOKES WITH
PARMIGIANO-REGGIANO MAYONNAISE

This is nice with larger artichokes as well. Trim off the tips and coarse leaves;
add 5 to 10 minutes to the cooking time, depending on the size.

8 baby artichokes

Parmigiano-Reggiano Mayonnaise
1/2 lemon
1 clove garlic, peeled
1 tablespoon fresh lemon juice
1 egg yolk
1/2 cup extra virgin olive oil
3 tablespoons grated Parmigiano-Reggiano
Salt and freshly ground white pepper to taste
1/4 teaspoon saffron threads (optional)
1 tablespoon very hot water

3 tablespoons capers, drained

To prepare the artichokes: Trim the tops of the artichokes. Remove the coarse outer leaves. Cut the base of the artichokes flat so they will stand upright. Rub all cut surfaces with the lemon. Place in a large pot with 2 inches of water. Squeeze the lemon half over the artichokes and drop the lemon into the water. Simmer, covered, for 10 to 12 minutes or until tender and the leaves can be removed with gentle pressure. Drain and refrigerate until ready to serve.

To make the mayonnaise: With the food processor (or blender) running, drop in the garlic clove. When minced, add the lemon juice and egg yolk. Blend, scraping the sides of the container occasionally. With the machine running, slowly drizzle in the olive oil.

Soak the saffron in the hot water for 2 minutes. Stir the Parmigiano-Reggiano and saffron-infused water into the mayonnaise; season with salt and pepper. Cover and refrigerate until ready to use.

Place the chilled artichokes upright on a serving platter, spreading the leaves slightly open. Spoon (or pipe with a pastry bag) the mayonnaise between the leaves of the artichokes. Sprinkle with the capers. *Serves 8*

Fava Beans in
Raspberry-Chardonnay Vinaigrette

*The creamy flavor of a nicely aged Chardonnay marries superbly with
rich, buttery fava beans and enhances the sparkle of Parmigiano. Leave some of
the smaller beans unpeeled; the peel is edible and adds interest to the salad.*

2 pounds very fresh fava beans, shelled

1 turnip or small jicama, peeled and diced

3 shallots, peeled and minced

3 tablespoons raspberry vinegar

2 tablespoons Chardonnay

1/2 cup safflower oil

Salt and freshly ground pepper to taste

1 teaspoon minced fresh flat-leaf parsley

6 radicchio leaves

2 ounces Parmigiano-Reggiano cheese, slivered

1/2 cup fresh raspberries (optional)

Blanch the fava beans in boiling water for 1 minute. Immerse in ice water to stop the cooking; drain. Set about one third of the smallest beans aside. Peel the remaining beans by pinching off the end and squeezing the brightly colored bean out.

Blanch the turnip (if using jicama, do not blanch) for 30 seconds in lightly salted boiling water; drain and immerse in ice water to stop the cooking and set the color.

In a medium non-reactive bowl, whisk together the shallots, raspberry vinegar, and Chardonnay. While continuously whisking, gradually drizzle in the oil. Season with salt and pepper and add the parsley.

Toss the vegetables with the vinaigrette and let stand for at least 15 minutes. Spoon into a radicchio leaf, sprinkle with the Parmigiano-Reggiano and a few raspberries, and serve. *Serves 6*

ASPARAGUS AND PARMIGIANO-REGGIANO
WRAPPED IN PROSCIUTTO

*The Italians have wonderful steaming pots just for asparagus. The spears are held
upright in a perforated container that allows the thicker end to be immersed in the water as the tips
simply steam. If you don't have one of these, just follow the instructions for blanching.*

1/2 pound asparagus (about 18 spears)
Eighteen 2-inch slivers of Parmigiano-Reggiano cheese
6 paper-thin slices prosciutto di Parma, chilled

Rinse the asparagus and cut off the root end. Trim
the base lightly with a vegetable peeler. To blanch,
drop in boiling salted water for 3 to 5 minutes,
depending on the thickness of the asparagus, until
crisp-tender. Drain and immediately immerse in
ice water to stop the cooking. When cool, drain
and pat dry.

With a very sharp knife, cut the chilled prosciutto into 1-inch-wide strips.

Bundle together a sliver of Parmigiano-
Reggiano and a spear of asparagus and bind them
with a strip of prosciutto. Repeat with remaining
Parmigiano-Reggiano and asparagus. Arrange on
a tray for passing. *Serves 6*

CARPACCIO

Ask your butcher to slice this beef for you so that it is ultra-thin.
It is much easier to handle when cold. Chill it before arranging it on the serving plates.

1 pound fillet of beef, sliced paper thin and chilled

1/4 cup extra virgin olive oil

1 tablespoon capers, drained

1/2 teaspoon sea salt, or to taste

1 tablespoon minced flat-leaf parsley

2 ounces Parmigiano-Reggiano cheese, shaved with
  a vegetable peeler

1 cup arugula leaves

1 lemon, cut into wedges

Freshly ground black pepper

Arrange the slices of beef on 6 chilled appetizer plates.

Combine the olive oil, capers, salt, and parsley and drizzle over each plate.

Place a large pinch of Parmigiano-Reggiano shavings in the center of each serving.

Place a few arugula leaves in the center of the cheese.

Serve with the lemon wedges and offer freshly ground black pepper. *Serves 6*

MARINATED MUSHROOM SALAD
WITH PARMIGIANO-REGGIANO SHARDS

Try marinating other seasonal vegetables in this marinade,
or serve it tossed with a salad of baby greens.

1 pound cultivated white mushrooms, stemmed

2 cloves garlic, peeled and minced

1/3 cup white wine vinegar

1 cup extra virgin olive oil

Salt and freshly ground pepper to taste

1 red bell pepper, seeded and cut into julienne

2 stalks celery, thinly sliced

1/4 cup minced flat-leaf parsley

4 ounces Parmigiano-Reggiano cheese,
  broken into 1/2-inch shards

Cut the mushroom caps in half and put in a non-reactive bowl.

In another bowl, combine the garlic and vinegar. Gradually whisk in the olive oil. Season with salt and pepper. Pour over the mushrooms and let stand at room temperature for 1 hour.

Cut the julienned red pepper into 1-inch lengths. Add the red pepper and celery to the mushrooms and toss well.

Add the parsley and Parmigiano-Reggiano to the mushrooms. Toss and place in serving bowl. Serve at room temperature. *Serves 6*

Radicchio Caesar Salad

Here's an unusual twist on a classic salad.
The traditional anchovy is omitted due to the strong flavor of the radicchio.
Serve this with the Parmigiano-Reggiano Croutons (opposite page).

4 heads radicchio
3 to 4 cloves garlic, peeled
1/2 cup extra virgin olive oil
2 tablespoons fresh lemon juice

1 teaspoon Worcestershire sauce
Salt and freshly ground pepper to taste
3 ounces Parmigiano-Reggiano cheese,
   shaved with a vegetable peeler

Rinse the radicchio leaves, spin dry, and tear into bite-sized pieces. Set aside.

In a blender or food processor, blend the garlic, olive oil, lemon juice, and Worcestershire sauce. Season with salt and pepper.

When ready to serve, toss with the radicchio leaves until well coated. Sprinkle the Parmigiano-Reggiano over the salad. *Serves 4*

PARMIGIANO-REGGIANO CROUTONS

Serve with salads or as an appetizer.
Delicious at the bottom of a soup bowl or as a topper.

1 baguette, cut into 1/2-inch slices
1/4 cup extra virgin olive oil

2 cloves garlic, peeled and minced
1 cup (4 ounces) coarsely grated Parmigiano-Reggiano

Preheat oven to 350°. Lightly oil a baking sheet.

Arrange the baguette slices on the prepared baking sheet.

In a small saucepan, heat the olive oil and garlic, but do not sauté. Remove from the heat and let stand for 15 minutes to infuse the oil with the garlic flavor.

Brush the oil lightly over the tops of the bread slices. Sprinkle the Parmigiano-Reggiano liberally over the bread. Bake in oven for 20 to 23 minutes, or until the cheese is melted and lightly browned. Let cool. *Makes about 3 dozen croutons*

A Marriage of Flavors

The marriage of some flavors can work magic in your mouth. Parmigiano, toasted walnuts, and balsamic vinegars are naturals, especially when their mellow flavors are contrasted with the sweet crispness of fennel and the brilliance of citrus.

FENNEL, BLOOD ORANGE, AND TOASTED WALNUT SALAD WITH PARMIGIANO-REGGIANO SHAVINGS

This refreshing winter salad is a great starter.
In larger portions it can be served for a luncheon main course.

8 ripe blood oranges

1 large fennel bulb, trimmed and finely sliced

4 leaves Bibb lettuce

1/4 cup extra virgin olive oil

1 tablespoon balsamic vinegar

Salt and freshly ground black pepper to taste

1/2 cup walnut halves, toasted (see page 106)

3 ounces Parmigiano-Reggiano cheese, shaved with
   a vegetable peeler

Cut off the top and bottom of the oranges down to the flesh. Stand each orange on end and cut off the peel down to the flesh with a large sharp knife, removing as much of the white pith as possible. Cut vertically along the membranes, to free the segments of orange. Put the segments in a medium bowl, adding any juice from the cutting board.

Add the fennel to the oranges and toss gently. Arrange the lettuce leaves on salad plates and spoon on the orange and fennel mixture.

Mix the oil and vinegar together and season with salt and pepper. Drizzle over the oranges and fennel. Place a few walnut pieces and Parmigiano-Reggiano shavings on each serving. *Serves 4*

PARMIGIANO-REGGIANO STUFFED
PORTOBELLO MUSHROOMS

*This hearty starter can also stand in as a vegetarian main dish.
It is also excellent grilled; just place under the broiler for a couple of
minutes to melt the Parmigiano topping.*

4 portobello mushrooms, 2 to 3 inches in diameter,
   stemmed

1/4 cup (1/2 ounce) dried porcini

21/4 cups chicken stock, heated (see page 105)

3 tablespoons extra virgin olive oil

3 shallots, peeled and minced

3 cloves garlic, peeled and minced

1 carrot, peeled and grated

11/3 cups couscous

1 cup (4 ounces) grated Parmigiano-Reggiano cheese

Salt and freshly ground pepper to taste

1/2 cup mixed minced herbs (parsley, thyme, oregano,
   marjoram, and/or rosemary)

Preheat the oven to 400°. Lightly oil a baking sheet.

Remove the dark gills from the mushroom caps. Place the caps on the prepared baking sheet.

Soak the porcini in the chicken stock for 15 minutes. Drain and chop, reserving the soaking liquid.

In a medium sauté pan, heat the olive oil over medium heat. Sauté shallots and garlic until softened, about 2 minutes. Add the carrot and chopped porcini. Strain and add reserved soaking liquid. Bring to a boil, reduce heat to a simmer, and cook for 4 to 5 minutes, or until the carrot is tender.

Add the couscous and remove from the heat. Cover and let stand for 5 minutes. Fluff with a fork and stir in 1/2 cup of the Parmigiano-Reggiano. Season with salt and pepper.

Spoon the mixture into the mushroom caps.

Combine the remaining Parmigiano-Reggiano with the herb mixture and sprinkle over the mushrooms. Bake for 20 to 25 minutes, or until golden brown. *Serves 4*

Minestra di Farro

What do the Italians do with the Parmigiano rind when all of the cheese is grated away? I once found a piece in the hand of a friend's child who was teething, but more often it is tossed into a simmering soup like this one to add body and flavor. Farro is an ancient strain of wheat, high in protein and nutty in taste. Look for it in natural food stores, or specialty mail-order catalogs.

1 cup borlotti beans (or dry bean of your choice)

Sprig of rosemary

1 clove garlic, peeled

1 cup whole farro

1/4 cup olive oil

1 onion, peeled and finely chopped

1 large carrot, peeled and finely chopped

1 stalk celery, finely chopped

6 to 7 cups chicken stock (see page 105)

3-inch piece of Parmigiano-Reggiano rind

2 cloves garlic, peeled and minced

Salt and freshly ground pepper to taste

1/4 cup minced flat-leaf parsley

Extra virgin olive oil for garnish

Soak the beans overnight with the rosemary and the whole clove of garlic.

In another bowl, soak the farro in water to cover overnight.

In a stockpot, heat the olive oil over medium heat, and sauté the onion, carrot, and celery over medium heat until onion begins to caramelize, about 5 minutes. Add the chicken stock and bring to a boil. Drain and stir in the soaked beans and the cheese rind; reduce heat to a simmer.

Cover and simmer for 1 hour. Add the minced garlic and farro. Continue to cook until beans are tender and the farro is creamy, about 1 to 1 1/2 hours longer. Add more chicken stock if necessary to maintain a soupy consistency.

Season with salt and pepper. Remove any remaining rind. Serve the soup with garnish of parsley and a drizzle of olive oil on top. *Serves 6*

Side dishes

ITALIAN RUBY CHARD CUSTARD

This recipe lends itself well to variations.
Try fresh spinach, beet greens, or broccoli florets in place of the red chard.

$1/4$ cup extra virgin olive oil

1 sweet red or yellow onion, peeled and chopped

2 pounds red Swiss chard, stems removed and discarded,
  and leaves cut into julienne

$3/4$ cup milk

4 eggs

1 cup (4 ounces) grated Parmigiano-Reggiano cheese

$1/8$ teaspoon freshly grated nutmeg

Salt and freshly ground pepper to taste

Preheat the oven to 375°. Lightly oil eight $1/2$-cup ramekins and place on a baking sheet.

In a sauté pan over medium heat, heat the olive oil and sauté the onion until softened, but not browned, about 3 minutes. Add the chard and cook until tender, about 4 to 5 minutes.

In a blender or food processor combine the chard mixture and the milk. Purée until smooth. Let cool.

Beat the eggs into the chard mixture. Add the Parmigiano-Reggiano, nutmeg, salt, and pepper. Pour into the prepared ramekins.

Bake for 30 to 35 minutes, or until a knife inserted in the center of each custard comes out clean. Serve at once in ramekins. *Serves 8*

SPINACH FLORENTINE

*Because this classic side dish can be prepared ahead, it's great for entertaining.
Keep it tightly covered until ready to reheat and serve.*

2 tablespoons unsalted butter
3 tablespoons all-purpose flour
1 1/4 cups milk heated with a bay leaf
1/4 cup extra virgin olive oil
2 cloves garlic, peeled and minced
1 pound fresh spinach, stemmed, washed, and chopped
Salt and freshly ground pepper to taste
2/3 cup (3 ounces) grated Parmigiano-Reggiano cheese

Preheat the oven to 350°. Lightly oil a 13 x 9-inch baking dish.

In a heavy, medium saucepan, melt the butter over medium heat. Whisk in the flour and cook, whisking constantly, for 2 to 3 minutes, until well incorporated. Remove bay leaf from heated milk and add the milk to the saucepan, whisking until smooth. Simmer for 8 to 10 minutes, or until slightly thickened.

In a large sauté pan over medium heat, heat the olive oil and sauté the garlic until softened, but not browned, about 2 minutes. Add the spinach and sauté until all of its water has evaporated, about 5 to 7 minutes. Season with salt and pepper.

Remove 1/4 cup of the sauce from the saucepan and set aside. Add the spinach mixture to the saucepan and blend well. Pour into the prepared baking dish.

Stir the Parmigiano-Reggiano into the reserved 1/4 cup sauce and pour over the top of the spinach mixture.

Bake for 15 minutes, or until heated through. Serve at once. *Serves 6*

EMILIO'S PARMIGIANO-REGGIANO FRICO CORNUCOPIAS

*This recipe was inspired by Lidia Bastianich, of the restaurant Felidia in
New York. Her original uses Montasio cheese, but chef Pete Clements at Emilio's Ristorante
in Santa Barbara makes a Parmigiano version. If your local cookware store
doesn't have cone-shaped cream-horn molds, you can make a stacked Napoleon. Simply cut
3-inch squares from the melted Parmigiano and rebake them flat. Layer three
of the squares with the spinach salad.*

2 cups (8 ounces) coarsely shredded
   Parmigiano-Reggiano cheese
3 cups julienned fresh spinach
2 red bell peppers, roasted, peeled, seeded, and
   cut julienne (see page 106)
1/3 cup finely chopped fresh basil
6 ounces goat cheese, crumbled
1 tablespoon balsamic vinegar
3 tablespoons extra virgin olive oil
Salt and freshly ground pepper to taste

Preheat the oven to 375°. Line a baking sheet with parchment paper.

Spread the Parmigiano-Reggiano evenly onto the prepared pan and place in the oven for 5 minutes, or until cheese has melted into one solid piece. Let cool slightly. While still warm, working quickly, cut the cheese into 6-inch squares and wrap each around a cone-shaped cream-horn mold.

Line the baking sheet with fresh paper. Place the molds upright on the pan and return to the oven to crisp for 8 to 10 minutes, until golden. Do not brown or the cheese will be bitter. Let the cones cool on the pan until ready to serve.

Just before serving, toss together the spinach, red pepper, basil, and goat cheese. Drizzle with balsamic vinegar and olive oil and toss to coat well. Season with salt and pepper. Stuff loosely into Parmigiano-Reggiano cones with a fork. Serve at once. *Serves 6*

ZUCCHINI FLOWERS STUFFED WITH
PARMIGIANO-REGGIANO AND RICOTTA

Zucchini flowers are easy to grow and are often found in specialty food stores or your farmers' market. If they are unavailable, substitute Swiss chard or large spinach leaves, twisting them into little pouches.

2 pounds baby zucchini, stems removed

16 zucchini flowers

1/2 cup ricotta cheese

1/2 cup (2 ounces) finely grated
   Parmigiano-Reggiano cheese

1 teaspoon minced fresh thyme

1 tablespoon minced fresh flat-leaf parsley

1 teaspoon minced fresh mint

Salt and freshly ground pepper to taste

Preheat the oven to 400°. Lightly oil a baking sheet.

Blanch the zucchini for 30 seconds in salted boiling water. Drain and immediately immerse in ice water to stop the cooking. Drain and place on the prepared baking sheet; set aside.

Gently rinse the inside of the zucchini flowers. Blanch them in boiling water for 5 seconds, or just long enough to soften. Drain and immediately immerse in ice water to stop the cooking. Drain at once and dry on paper towels.

Mix the ricotta, Parmigiano-Reggiano, and herbs together until blended. Place the mixture in a pastry bag.

Fill each flower with the cheese mixture. Twist the ends slightly and place with the baby zucchini on the prepared baking sheet. Season with salt and freshly ground pepper.

Cover tightly with aluminum foil and bake for 10 minutes, or just until heated through. Do not overcook.

Place the baby zucchini on a warmed serving platter. Arrange the zucchini flowers on top. Serve at once. *Serves 8*

ROMA TOMATOES STUFFED WITH
PARMIGIANO-REGGIANO RISOTTO

This is a great dish for summer, when tomatoes are full of flavor. For a hearty winter
main dish, try stuffing half a baked butternut squash with the risotto.

8 ripe Roma tomatoes, cut into halves, lengthwise

1/4 cup plus 2 tablespoons extra virgin olive oil

1 onion, peeled and diced

1 cup Carnaroli rice (or your choice of Italian rice)

1/4 cup dry white wine

5 to 6 cups rich chicken stock, heated (see page 105)

2 teaspoons minced fresh thyme

Salt and freshly ground pepper to taste

1/2 cup (2 ounces) grated Parmigiano-Reggiano cheese

1/4 cup julienned fresh basil leaves for garnish

Preheat the oven to 300°.

Scoop the pulp out of the tomatoes. Chop and reserve the pulp. Arrange the tomatoes on a baking sheet cut side up.

In a heavy saucepan over medium heat, heat the 1/4 cup oil and sauté the onion until softened, but not browned, about 3 minutes. Add the rice and stir to coat with the oil, stirring until opaque, about 3 to 4 minutes. Add the white wine and stir until absorbed.

Add the heated chicken stock 1 cup at a time, always stirring, and always keeping enough liquid on the rice to keep it moist. Continue cooking over medium heat until rice is al dente, about 15 to 20 minutes. Add the reserved tomato pulp, the thyme, and the remaining 2 tablespoons olive oil. Season with salt and pepper.

Scoop the mixture into the tomato halves and bake for about 10 minutes, or until just heated through. Don't leave them in the oven too long or the risotto will dry out and tomato will begin to cook. Top with the Parmigiano-Reggiano. Place under the broiler until cheese is lightly browned, about 2 minutes. Transfer to a warmed serving platter. Sprinkle with the julienned basil and serve at once. *Serves 8*

CARAMELIZED ONION AND APPLE TART

This sweet and savory tart goes well with roasted pork and poultry dishes.
It could also be served as an appetizer or first course.

Pastry

1/2 cup (1 stick) cold unsalted butter

1 1/4 cups all-purpose flour

1/2 teaspoon salt

4 to 5 tablespoons ice water

Onion and Apple Filling

1/3 cup extra virgin olive oil

2 large red sweet onions, thinly sliced

1/4 cup (3 ounces) minced pancetta (optional)

1/2 cup apple juice

1 Rome apple, peeled, cored, and diced

3 pippin or Granny Smith apples

1 cup milk

2 eggs

1 teaspoon ground coriander

3/4 cup (3 ounces) grated Parmigiano-Reggiano cheese

To make the pastry: Cut the butter into tablespoon-sized pieces. In a food processor, combine the flour and salt. With the machine running, drop in 1 piece of butter at a time, processing until evenly distributed. Pulse, adding water just until the dough comes together. Do not overprocess, or the dough will be tough. Place in plastic wrap and flatten into a disk shape. Refrigerate for at least 1 hour.

Preheat the oven to 350°.

On a lightly floured work surface, roll the dough out to a thickness of 1/4 inch. Fit the dough into a 10-inch tart pan with a removable bottom. Line with parchment paper and fill with pastry weights. Bake for 35 minutes, or until firm and lightly colored. Place on a wire rack to cool slightly.

To make the filling: In a sauté pan over medium-high heat, heat the olive oil and sauté the onions and pancetta until lightly browned, about 8 to 10 minutes. Deglaze the pan with the apple juice, scraping the sides to loosen particles of cooked-on onion. Bring to a boil.

Add the diced Rome apple to the pan, lower heat to a simmer, and cook until the apple is falling-apart tender and the liquid is reduced, about 10 to 15 minutes. Let cool.

Peel, core, and slice the pippin apples.

In a bowl, beat the milk, eggs, and coriander together. Stir into cooled apple-onion mixture. Fold in the sliced apples and pour into the pastry shell.

Top with Parmigiano-Reggiano. Bake for 25 to 30 minutes, or until the cheese is golden brown and a knife inserted in the center comes out clean. Transfer to a wire rack and let cool slightly before cutting. *Serves 8*

GRILLED PARMIGIANO POLENTA ROUNDS

*This is a great accompaniment
to most meats. It also makes a nice
first course, served with
Zesty Tomato Sauce (page 105).*

4 1/2 cups chicken stock (see page 105)
1 1/2 cups polenta
1/2 cup (2 ounces) grated Parmigiano-Reggiano cheese

Preheat the oven to 375°. Lightly oil a baking sheet.

In a large saucepan, bring the chicken stock to a boil. Gradually whisk in the polenta, whisking constantly. Lower the heat to medium and cook, stirring constantly for about 20 minutes, or until the polenta comes easily away from the side of the pot.

Spread the polenta evenly into the prepared baking sheet and smooth the top. Sprinkle with the Parmigiano-Reggiano and bake for 15 minutes, or until the cheese is melted and lightly browned. Let cool.

With a 2-inch biscuit cutter, cut out rounds from the polenta. With a metal spatula, transfer the rounds to a plate until ready to grill.

Grill, cheese-side up, for 3 to 4 minutes, until heated through. Do not turn. Serve immediately. *Serves 8*

GARLIC AND PARMIGIANO MASHED POTATOES

*You can't just roast one head
of garlic. . . . I always make extra to use as
a garnish, to spread on bread, to flavor salad
dressings, or just to snack on while I'm
waiting for guests. For an extra garlic boost,
use the oil left from roasting the garlic in
place of the olive oil in this recipe.*

4 large baking potatoes
1 head roasted garlic (see page 106)
1 cup milk, heated
2 tablespoons extra virgin olive oil
1 cup (4 ounces) coarsely grated
   Parmigiano-Reggiano cheese
Salt and freshly ground pepper to taste

Peel the potatoes and cut them into 2-inch chunks. Put in a large saucepan and cover with cold water. Bring to a boil and cook until fork tender, about 20 minutes. Drain thoroughly. Pass through a ricer or food mill and return to the saucepan.

Squeeze the roasted garlic cloves from the skin and mash. Set aside.

Add the milk, olive oil, Parmigiano-Reggiano, and roasted garlic to the potatoes, stirring over low heat to warm. Season with salt and pepper. Transfer immediately to warmed serving dishes and serve. *Serves 4*

Parmigiano:
An Excellent Finish

*Molière, the famous
seventeenth-century
French playwright, is
reputed to have lived
only on Parmesan cheese
and wine at the end of
his life, a trend adopted
by many of his
acquaintances. He was
quoted as saying, "Ah,
no, my wife's broths are
truly nitric acid to me;
you know all the
ingredients she has put
into them. Rather, let me
have a small piece of
Parmesan cheese."*

1994

Pasta

SPAGHETTI CARBONARA

*Pancetta is a classic ingredient in this dish, but if you have trouble
finding it, just substitute the same amount of bacon.*

2 tablespoons extra virgin olive oil
1 onion, diced
4 ounces pancetta, diced
1 pound spaghetti
4 egg yolks, beaten
1/2 cup heavy cream
1 cup (4 ounces) grated Parmigiano-Reggiano cheese
Salt and freshly ground pepper
3 tablespoons minced fresh flat-leaf parsley

In a small sauté pan over medium heat, heat olive oil and sauté the onion until softened, but not browned, about 3 minutes. Add the pancetta and cook until lightly browned. Set aside to cool slightly.

In a large pot of salted boiling water, cook the spaghetti for 8 to 10 minutes, or until al dente. In a large bowl, beat the egg yolks, cream, and Parmigiano-Reggiano together. Add the cooled onion mixture and season with salt and pepper.

Drain the spaghetti and toss with the egg mixture until well coated. Turn into warmed serving bowl, sprinkle with parsley, and serve immediately. *Serves 6*

Penne with Roasted Beets and Beet Greens

*Roasting vegetables sweetens them, and the flavor of beets
is especially enhanced by this process. The beets also add strong visual interest:
when mixed with the pasta the color of this dish is an appealing fuschia.*

1 bunch (about 8) small or 3 large beets with greens
1/4 cup extra virgin olive oil
Salt and freshly ground pepper to taste
1 pound penne pasta
1 onion, peeled and finely chopped
3/4 cup (3 ounces) coarsely shredded
  Parmigiano-Reggiano cheese

Preheat the oven to 400°. Lightly oil a medium casserole.

Remove the beet leaves and discard the tough stems. Rinse and spin dry; julienne the leaves and set aside. Trim the root and stem from the beets and scrub well. If using large beets, cut into quarters. Drop into boiling water and cook for 15 minutes, or until tender when pierced with a fork. Drain, reserving the water, and remove the skins. Place the beets in the prepared casserole and drizzle with 2 tablespoons of the olive oil. Season with salt and pepper. Roast in the oven (or over a grill for a smoky flavor) for 20 minutes, or until lightly browned.

In a large pot of salted boiling water, cook the pasta until al dente, about 8 to 10 minutes.

Meanwhile, in a medium sauté pan heat the remaining 2 tablespoons olive oil over medium heat and sauté the onion until golden brown, about 3 to 4 minutes. Add 1 cup of the reserved beet-cooking water and bring to a boil. Cook to reduce the volume by half. Add the julienned beet greens and cook just until wilted.

In a large serving dish, combine the roasted beets, greens, and pasta. Sprinkle with the Parmigiano-Reggiano and serve at once. *Serves 4*

FUSILLI WITH NEW POTATOES, OVEN-DRIED TOMATOES, AND WHITE BEANS

Timing is everything in this recipe. I use my toaster oven to roast the potatoes while drying the tomatoes in my regular oven. If you don't have a second oven, cook the potatoes on top of the stove and finish them under the broiler just before serving.

1 cup dried cannellini beans

1 tablespoon minced fresh rosemary plus
   1 sprig rosemary

3 tablespoons plus 1/4 cup extra virgin olive oil

1 onion, finely chopped

1 carrot, peeled and finely chopped

1 stalk celery, finely chopped

5 cups rich chicken stock (see page 105)

6 Roma tomatoes, cut into quarters lengthwise

Sea salt to taste

1 pound new red potatoes, scrubbed and
   cut into 2-inch chunks

1/2 pound curly fusilli pasta

1/2 cup (2 ounces) Parmigiano-Reggiano cheese chips

Soak the beans overnight in water to cover, with the minced rosemary.

Preheat the oven to 250°

In a large saucepan over medium heat, heat the 3 tablespoons oil and sauté the onion, carrot, and celery until golden brown, about 6 to 8 minutes. Add the chicken stock and drained beans. Bring to a boil, then reduce to a simmer. Add rosemary sprig and cook, uncovered, at a simmer for approximately 2 hours, or until beans are tender but not falling apart.

Meanwhile, place the tomatoes, cut side up, on a wire rack on a baking sheet. Sprinkle with sea salt and put in the warmed oven for approximately 2 hours. Tomatoes will dehydrate and intensify in flavor, but still be a little soft.

Remove the tomatoes from the oven and increase the oven temperature to 400°.

Toss the potatoes with the remaining olive oil and season liberally with sea salt. Place in a roasting dish and roast, turning occasionally, for 40 to 45 minutes, or until easily pierced with a fork and the cut edges are golden brown.

When the beans, tomatoes, and potatoes are all done, cook the pasta in a large pot of salted boiling water until al dente, about 8 to 10 minutes. Drain well and place in a large bowl. Add the beans and their cooking liquid and the potatoes. Add the tomatoes and sprinkle the Parmigiano-Reggiano chips over the top. Serve at once. *Serves 6 to 8*

TRENNE WITH CARAMELIZED ONIONS, LEMON ZEST, AND CAPERS

Trenne is a triangular-shaped tube pasta imported from Abruzzi. Any short, stocky pasta can be used in this dish, which is delicious served with grilled seafood or chicken.

1/4 cup olive oil

2 large onions, peeled and thinly sliced

2 teaspoons lemon zest

2 cloves garlic, minced

Juice of 1 lemon

1 cup chicken stock (see page 105)

1 pound trenne pasta

2 tablespoons capers, drained

1/4 cup minced fresh flat-leaf parsley

Salt and freshly ground pepper to taste

1/4 cup (1 ounce) grated Parmigiano-Reggiano cheese

In a large skillet over medium heat, heat the olive oil and sauté the onions until golden, about 6 to 8 minutes. Add the lemon zest and garlic and cook until softened, about 2 to 3 minutes. Deglaze the pan with the lemon juice. Reduce heat to a simmer and add the chicken stock. Continue to cook uncovered over low heat for 10 minutes, until slightly reduced.

Meanwhile, in a large pot of salted boiling water, cook the pasta, until al dente, about 6 to 8 minutes. Toss with the onion mixture; add the capers, parsley, salt, and pepper. Serve immediately, with the Parmigiano-Reggiano sprinkled on top. *Serves 4*

BASIL GNOCCHI WITH PESTO

Potatoes become glutinous when over-mashed. A ricer or food mill makes this job a lot easier.
If you don't have one, finely chop the potato with a sharp knife.

1 1/2 pounds baking potatoes, peeled and
   cut into 2-inch pieces
2 cups all-purpose flour
1 teaspoon salt
1/2 cup firmly packed fresh basil leaves
2 eggs, beaten
1/2 cup pesto (see page 106)
3 to 5 tablespoons olive oil
Freshly grated Parmigiano-Reggiano cheese for serving

In a large saucepan, cook the potatoes in salted boiling water until tender, about 20 minutes. Drain and put through a ricer or food mill.

Place the flour in a food processor and add the salt and basil leaves. Process until finely incorporated. Transfer to a large bowl.

Make a well in the center of the flour and add the potatoes and eggs. Knead until soft and smooth. Divide the dough into 4 pieces and, on a floured surface, roll each into a sausage shape about 1/2 inch in diameter. Cut into 1-inch lengths. Dust lightly with flour and press against the tines of a fork while making a small indentation with your finger on the other side. Set aside on a lightly floured surface until ready to cook.

Cook the gnocchi in salted boiling water for 3 to 5 minutes, or until tender but still slightly firm. Drain and toss with the pesto, and olive oil, if needed. Serve at once with the Parmigiano-Reggiano. *Serves 6*

SPINACH-RICOTTA PASTA HANDKERCHIEFS
WITH BROWNED BUTTER AND SAGE

This classic northern Italian pasta is easy to make.
If you don't have time to make fresh pasta dough, try using wonton skins!

1 pound fresh spinach, stemmed and rinsed

1 cup ricotta cheese

1/2 cup (2 ounces) finely grated
  Parmigiano-Reggiano cheese

1 egg, separated

1/4 teaspoon freshly grated nutmeg

Salt and freshly ground pepper to taste

1 pound fresh pasta dough (see page 104)

20 fresh sage leaves

1/2 cup (1 stick) unsalted butter

2 tablespoons extra virgin olive oil

1/4 cup (1 ounce) coarsely grated
  Parmigiano-Reggiano cheese

Steam the spinach, covered, over boiling water for 2 minutes, or until wilted. Let cool slightly and squeeze as dry as possible. Chop the spinach very finely.

In a medium bowl, combine the spinach, ricotta, and the 1/2 cup finely grated Parmigiano-Reggiano. Add the egg yolk, nutmeg, salt and pepper, and mix well.

Roll pasta dough out and cut it into 3-inch squares. Pipe or spoon 1 teaspoon of the spinach mixture on each square. Brush the edges of each square with egg white and fold into a triangle, sealing the edges well. In a large pot of salted boiling water cook the filled pasta for 2 minutes, or until al dente. Drain and place in a warmed serving bowl.

Reserve 8 sage leaves for garnish and julienne the remaining leaves. In a medium saucepan, melt the butter over medium heat until it foams. Add the olive oil and julienned sage leaves. Cook over medium heat until the butter is golden brown—do not burn it! Pour over the ravioli, add the Parmigiano-Reggiano, and toss gently. Garnish with the whole sage leaves and serve at once. *Serves 8*

WHITE-WHITE-WHITE
WHITE ASPARAGUS RISOTTO WITH WHITE TRUFFLES

*White asparagus and truffles make an elegant risotto, but they are not
always available. Substitute green asparagus or a vegetable of your choice, and if you
can get white truffle oil, it is a terrific substitute for the real thing.*

1 1/2 pounds white asparagus, peeled

7 1/2 to 8 cups chicken stock (see page 105)

1/4 cup extra virgin olive oil

1 onion, peeled and diced

1 1/4 cups Carnaroli rice (or your choice of Italian rice)

1/4 cup dry white wine

1 teaspoon finely grated lemon zest

1/2 cup (2 ounces) grated Parmigiano-Reggiano cheese,
   plus more for serving

2 tablespoons unsalted butter

Salt and freshly ground pepper to taste

1/2 ounce white truffle, shaved, or 1 tablespoon
   white truffle oil (optional)

Cut off the top 2 inches of the asparagus, reserving the stems. Blanch the tips in salted boiling water for 1 minute. Drain and immediately immerse in ice water to stop the cooking. Drain and set aside.

Bring the chicken stock to a boil and cook the stems until very tender, about 10 to 12 minutes. Using a slotted spoon, transfer the stems to a blender. Add 1/2 cup of the stock and purée. Strain through a fine-meshed sieve to remove any tough fiber and return the purée to the chicken stock, keeping it at a simmer.

In a medium saucepan over a medium heat, heat the 1/4 cup olive oil and sauté the onion until softened, but not browned, about 3 minutes. Add the rice and stir to coat with the oil, stirring until the rice is opaque, about 3 to 4 minutes. Add the white wine and lemon zest; stir until the wine is absorbed.

Add the heated asparagus-stock mixture 1 cup at a time, always stirring, and always keeping enough liquid on the rice to keep it moist. Continue cooking over medium heat until the rice is al dente. This should take 15 to 20 minutes.

Add the asparagus tips and Parmigiano-Reggiano. Stir in the butter. Season with salt and pepper. If using truffle oil, add it now.

Sprinkle the white truffle shavings over the top when serving. Serve with additional Parmigiano-Reggiano. *Serves 6*

**A Cheese for
All Seasons**

*Fall is a special time
in Italy. Along with the
harvest of grapes and
olives, wild mushrooms
pop up, begging to be
gathered. Weather and
food work together to
create a classic picture of
comfort: meats roasting
over a crackling fire, fresh
peppery olive oil drizzled
over grilled Tuscan bread,
and a glass of Amarone
to be sipped while
nibbling on shards of
Parmigiano-Reggiano.*

WILD MUSHROOM LASAGNE

*This dish is heavenly when made with fresh pasta. If you don't
have time to make your own, some stores sell fresh pasta sheets. Failing that, it is
still delicious made with a box of dried lasagna noodles.*

1 pound fresh pasta dough (see recipe page 104)

1/2 cup (1 stick) unsalted butter

6 tablespoons all-purpose flour

3 cups milk, heated with 1 bay leaf

Freshly ground nutmeg

Salt and freshly ground white pepper to taste

1/4 cup (1/2 ounce) dried porcini mushrooms

1 cup veal stock or chicken stock (see page 105), heated

1 pound white cultivated mushrooms

1 pound assorted fresh wild mushrooms (shiitake, portobello, oyster, chanterelle)

1/4 cup extra virgin olive oil

4 cloves garlic, peeled and minced

2 yellow bell peppers, roasted, seeded, peeled, and cut into julienne (see page 106)

1/4 cup minced fresh flat-leaf parsley

2 teaspoons minced fresh thyme

1 cup (4 ounces) grated Parmigiano-Reggiano cheese

Preheat the oven to 350°. Lightly oil a 13 x 9-inch baking dish.

Cut the fresh pasta into strips to fit baking dish. In a large pot of salted boiling water, cook the pasta until al dente, about 3 minutes. Drain and set aside in a bowl of cool water until ready to assemble lasagne.

In a medium, heavy saucepan, melt the butter over medium heat. Add the flour and cook, whisking constantly, for 2 to 3 minutes. Gradually whisk in the heated milk, removing bay leaf, and whisk until smooth. Simmer for 10 minutes, or until thickened. Season with nutmeg, salt, and white pepper.

Soak the dried porcini for 20 minutes in the stock. Strain, reserving soaking liquid. Chop the porcini and add to the sauce.

Remove the stems from fresh mushrooms and julienne the caps.

In a large sauté pan, heat the olive oil over medium heat and sauté the garlic until softened, about 2 minutes. Add the fresh mushrooms and cook until softened, about 5 minutes. Add the yellow peppers, parsley, and thyme; mix well. Add the reserved mushroom-soaking liquid and cook until thickened, about 5 minutes more. Season with salt and pepper to taste.

Spread a little of the white sauce on the bottom of the baking dish. Layer the pasta, white sauce, and mushrooms, repeating to finish with a top layer of the white sauce. Sprinkle with Parmigiano-Reggiano and bake for 45 minutes, or until top is golden brown. *Serves 8*

Main
dishes

GRILLED EGGPLANT PARMIGIANO

If tomatoes are not in season, use canned ones. They are picked ripe and packed immediately, so the flavor is much better than that of off-season fresh tomatoes. When buying canned tomatoes, get a 28-ounce can of whole tomatoes. Drain and chop them, reserving the liquid to add back in. If fresh herbs are not available, substitute one third as much dried herb.

1 large eggplant, peeled and cut into
  1/2-inch-thick slices

Sea salt for dehydrating eggplant

Extra virgin olive oil for brushing, plus 2 tablespoons

2 cloves garlic, peeled and minced

6 large ripe tomatoes, peeled and chopped (see page
  106)

1/4 cup fresh basil leaves, minced

1 tablespoon minced fresh flat-leaf parsley

1 teaspoon minced fresh mint

Salt and freshly ground pepper to taste

1/2 cup (2 ounces) grated Parmigiano-Reggiano cheese

Sprinkle the eggplant with sea salt on both sides and let drain for 30 minutes on a wire rack. Preheat a grill or broiler. Lightly oil an 8-inch square casserole.

Rinse off the eggplant and pat dry with paper towels. Brush lightly with olive oil. Grill or broil the eggplant on both sides until lightly browned.

Preheat the oven to 350°.

In a large saucepan over medium heat, heat the 2 tablespoons olive oil and sauté the garlic for 2 minutes, or until softened. Add the tomatoes and herbs and cook over medium heat for 10 to 15 minutes, just to thicken slightly. Season with salt and pepper to taste.

Spoon half of the tomato sauce into the prepared casserole. Place the eggplant in a single layer with the edges slightly overlapping. Cover with the remaining tomato sauce. Top with the Parmigiano-Reggiano and bake for 30 to 35 minutes, or until bubbling hot and the cheese is golden brown. *Serves 4*

GRILLED TUNA WITH WHITE BEAN AND PARMIGIANO-REGGIANO PUREÉ

Sometimes I make this dish and leave the beans whole. Any leftover bean purée makes a delicious topping for crostini or filling for ravioli.

1 cup dried cannellini beans

1 clove garlic

1 sprig rosemary

3 tablespoons extra virgin olive oil

1 onion, finely chopped

1 carrot, peeled and finely chopped

1 stalk celery, finely chopped

4 to 4 1/2 cups rich chicken stock (see page 105)

1 tablespoon minced fresh flat-leaf parsley plus
    4 sprigs for garnish

Salt and freshly ground white pepper

4 fresh tuna steaks (1 1/2 pounds total)

Olive oil for coating

3/4 cup (3 ounces) grated Parmigiano-Reggiano cheese

Soak the beans overnight in water to cover, with the garlic and rosemary.

In a large saucepan over medium heat, heat the oil and sauté the onion, carrot, and celery until golden brown. Add the chicken stock and drained beans. Bring to a boil, then reduce heat to a simmer. Cook, uncovered, for about 2 hours, or until the beans are very tender.

Preheat a grill or broiler.

Drain the beans, reserving the cooking liquid. Place the beans in a blender with 1/4 cup of the cooking liquid and purée. Add the parsley, salt, and white pepper. Return to the saucepan and keep warm, adding more cooking liquid if necessary.

Coat the tuna with olive oil and season with salt and pepper. Grill or broil for 4 to 5 minutes on each side, or until lightly browned on the outside, but still rare on the inside.

Add the Parmigiano-Reggiano to the bean purée. Add more cooking liquid to achieve the desired consistency. Spoon onto 4 warmed dinner plates and top with the grilled tuna. Garnish with the parsley sprigs. *Serves 4*

SAUTÉED LEMON-GARLIC PRAWNS WITH PARMIGIANO-REGGIANO CREAM SAUCE

Seafood is usually not combined with Parmigiano-Reggiano in Italy.
But this light sauce works well with the shrimp, and also with other meats and pasta.

16 prawns or jumbo shrimp, shelled and deveined
1/4 cup extra virgin olive oil
1/4 cup fresh lemon juice
1 teaspoon finely minced lemon zest
3 garlic cloves, minced
Salt and freshly ground pepper to taste
1 pound haricots verts or green beans, blanched

Parmigiano-Reggiano Cream Sauce

2 cups dry white wine
2 shallots, minced
2 cups chicken stock (see page 105)
1 cup heavy cream
2/3 cup (3 ounces) grated Parmigiano-Reggiano cheese
Salt and freshly ground white pepper to taste

Place the prawns in a shallow dish.

Combine the olive oil, lemon juice, lemon zest, and garlic. Mix well and pour over the prawns. Marinate in the refrigerator for at least 1 hour, or up to overnight.

In a large sauté pan over medium heat, heat 2 tablespoons of the marinade. Using a slotted spoon, transfer the shrimp to the pan and sauté for 4 to 5 minutes, or until prawns are pink. Season with salt and pepper. Add the haricots verts and toss to heat. Turn out onto a warmed serving platter and serve with Parmigiano-Reggiano Cream Sauce on the side.

To make the sauce: In a large saucepan, combine the wine and shallots. Cook over high heat until most of the liquid has evaporated. Add the chicken stock and cook over high heat until reduced by half.

Add the cream and cook until hot. Stir in the Parmigiano-Reggiano. Season with salt and pepper.
Serves 4

VEAL SCALOPPINE

This dish exemplifies a classic flavor combination that is simple and satisfying. Also try substituting turkey cutlets for the veal. It is delicious served with sautéed spinach.

4 veal cutlets, about 1 1/4 pounds

1 cup all-purpose flour

1/2 teaspoon garlic salt

1/4 teaspoon freshly ground pepper

2 eggs, beaten

1/2 cup (2 ounces) finely grated
    Parmigiano-Reggiano cheese

3 tablespoons unsalted butter

4 thin slices prosciutto di Parma, cut into 3-inch strips

1/4 cup (1 ounce) coarsely grated
    Parmigiano-Reggiano cheese

4 sprigs fresh flat-leaf parsley, minced

2 lemons, cut into wedges

Preheat the broiler. Lightly oil a baking sheet.

Roll the veal between 2 pieces of parchment paper with a rolling pin until flattened to an even thickness, about 1/8 inch. Cut each piece in half.

In a medium bowl, stir together the flour, garlic salt and pepper.

Dip the veal into the eggs, the finely grated Parmigiano-Reggiano, the eggs again, then the flour mixture.

In a large sauté pan, melt the butter over medium heat until it foams. Add the veal, and cook for about 1 minute per side, or until lightly browned. Transfer to the prepared baking sheet.

Place a strip of prosciutto on 4 of the cutlets. Sprinkle half of the coarsely grated Parmigiano-Reggiano over that and top with another cutlet. Sprinkle with the remaining cheese and place under the broiler for 3 to 4 minutes, or until top is browned and the cheese inside is melted.

Garnish with parsley and serve with lemon wedges. *Serves 4*

FRUIT STUFFED PORK LOIN ROASTED WITH FENNEL, POTATOES, AND GARLIC

This is fall comfort food. The apple and dried apricot mixture
is also an excellent stuffing for turkey or chicken.

1 boneless pork loin, trimmed (about 2 pounds)

Salt and freshly ground pepper to taste

1 Granny Smith or pippin apple, peeled,
   cored and diced

6 dried apricots, minced

1/2 cup (2 ounces) finely grated
   Parmigiano-Reggiano cheese

1 teaspoon minced fresh sage

4 tablespoons unsalted butter

3 fennel bulbs, trimmed and thinly sliced (reserve leaves
   for garnish)

2 pounds Yukon Gold or yellow Finn potatoes, scrubbed
   and cut in half

10 cloves garlic, peeled

2 tablespoons olive oil

Preheat the oven to 400°. Lightly oil a roasting pan.

Split the pork loin lengthwise without cutting completely through so that it can be opened like a book. Pound lightly to even thickness of about 1 inch. Season with salt and pepper.

Combine the apples, apricots, Parmigiano-Reggiano, and sage. Spread evenly inside the pork loin. Close the flaps to cover the stuffing and tie with kitchen twine at 2-inch intervals. Season the outside with salt and pepper.

In a large sauté pan, melt the butter over medium heat and cook until golden brown. Add the pork loin and lightly brown on all sides. Place in the prepared roasting pan.

Add the fennel, potatoes, and garlic cloves to the roasting pan. Drizzle the olive oil over the loin and vegetables. Roast in the oven for 35 to 45 minutes, or until an instant-read thermometer registers 160°.

Slice across the roll to serve. Transfer to warmed serving platter, add potatoes, fennel, and garlic. Garnish with reserved fennel fronds. *Serves 6*

PARMIGIANO-CRUSTED LEMON CHICKEN

This simple but delicious chicken recipe is great served on a bed of fettuccine with Parmigiano-Reggiano Cream Sauce (page 77). You can also substitute the lemon with orange. For a little extra flavor, add 1/2 teaspoon minced citrus zest to the sauce.

8 skinless, boneless chicken breast halves

Juice of 1 lemon

1 cup fresh bread crumbs

1/2 cup (2 ounces) finely grated Parmigiano-Reggiano cheese

1/2 cup walnuts, toasted and coarsely chopped (see page 106)

2 teaspoons finely grated lemon zest

1 tablespoon minced fresh flat-leaf parsley

1 teaspoon minced fresh thyme

1/2 teaspoon minced fresh rosemary

1/2 teaspoon minced fresh marjoram

1 teaspoon sea salt

1/2 teaspoon freshly ground pepper

2 large eggs beaten with 1 tablespoon milk

Flour for dredging

Preheat the oven to 375°. Lightly oil a 13 x 9-inch baking dish.

Place the chicken in a shallow dish and sprinkle both sides with lemon juice.

Spread the bread crumbs on a baking sheet and toast in the oven for 5 to 7 minutes, until golden brown. Let cool.

In a medium bowl, combine the Parmigiano-Reggiano, walnuts, lemon zest, parsley, thyme, rosemary, marjoram, salt and pepper. Add the toasted bread crumbs and mix well.

Dip each chicken breast into the beaten egg, dredge in the flour, dip in the egg again, and coat with the bread crumb mixture, pressing to coat well. Place in a single layer in the prepared baking dish and bake for 30 to 35 minutes, or until juices run clear when the breasts are pierced with a knife. Serve at once. *Serves 4*

SQUAB WITH ROASTED PEAR AND GARLIC

Cornish game hens or quail can be used in place of the squab.
Game hens will take longer, 35 to 45 minutes, and quail will take a little less.

8 squab

Salt and freshly ground pepper to taste

2 ripe pears, peeled, cored, and diced, plus 2 whole pears

1 cup (4 ounces) coarsely shredded
　Parmigiano-Reggiano cheese

2 cloves garlic, peeled and minced

1 teaspoon minced fresh sage

1 tablespoon minced fresh flat-leaf parsley

1 teaspoon fresh minced thyme

2 tablespoons unsalted butter, cut into bits

1/4 cup olive oil

1/4 cup dry white wine

2 cups chicken stock (page 105)

Preheat the oven to 375°.

Rinse the squab and pat dry. Sprinkle inside and out with salt and pepper. Mix together the diced pear, Parmigiano-Reggiano, garlic, sage, parsley, thyme, and butter. Stuff loosely into the birds. Close openings with toothpicks or skewers.

In a Dutch oven or large stovetop casserole over medium-high heat, heat the olive oil and brown the squab on all sides. Remove the squab from the pan and set aside. Deglaze the pan with the wine, stirring to loosen cooked bits from the pan. Add the chicken stock and cook over medium heat for 10 minutes, or until slightly reduced. Return the squab to the pan.

Peel, halve, and core the remaining 2 pears. Add them to the baking dish and roast, uncovered, for 25 to 30 minutes. Test for doneness by inserting a sharp knife into the thigh. If the juices are pink, it needs to cook longer. If the juices run clear, it is done.

Transfer the squab and pear halves to a serving platter. Strain the pan juices and serve on the side.
Serves 4

**Classic Flavor
Combination**

*The Italians of the
nineteenth century had a
proverb:* al contadino
non far sapere quanto
é buono il formaggio
con le pere *("never let
the peasant see how tasty
cheese is with pears").
It is a classic combination
that is hard to resist,
especially when sliced and
drizzled with another
of Emilia-Romagna's
artisanal products,
balsamic vinegar.*

Baked goods

POTATO FOCACCIA WITH RED ONIONS AND PARMIGIANO-REGGIANO

The liquid in this recipe is the water that the potatoes are cooked in.
Riced potatoes are added to the dough, and sliced potatoes are placed on top. If you don't
have a potato ricer or food mill, don't use a blender or food processor—simply chop
the potatoes with a sharp knife by hand as finely as possible.

3 russet potatoes
1 package active dry yeast
1 1/4 cups warm water (potato cooking liquid)
2 teaspoons sugar
3 1/2 to 4 cups all-purpose flour
1 teaspoon salt

Extra virgin olive oil for brushing
1 red onion, cut into 1/4-inch-thick slices
3/4 cup (3 ounces) coarsely grated
   Parmigiano-Reggiano cheese
1 tablespoon coarse sea salt
2 tablespoons minced fresh sage

Peel and cut 2 of the potatoes into 1-inch chunks. Put in a medium saucepan, cover with water, and boil until tender, about 20 minutes. Drain, reserving the cooking water. Pass the potatoes through a ricer or food mill.

Dissolve the yeast and sugar in 1/2 cup of the warm reserved potato-cooking water. Let stand for 5 minutes, or until foamy.

In a heavy-duty mixer with a dough hook, mix the flour, riced potatoes, and salt together. Add the yeast mixture and 3/4 cup of the remaining potato water and mix to make a soft dough, about 2 to 3 minutes. Transfer to a lightly floured work surface and knead until smooth and not sticky, about 3 to 4 minutes. Place in a lightly oiled bowl, cover, and let rise in a warm place until doubled, about 1 hour.

Lightly oil a baking sheet. Roll the dough out on a lightly floured work surface to fit the baking sheet. Place the dough on the sheet and let rise until doubled, about 30 minutes.

Preheat the oven to 425°.

Scrub the remaining potato and cut it into 1/4-inch-thick slices. Blanch the potato slices in boiling salted water for 2 to 3 minutes, until softened, but not falling apart.

Brush the top of the focaccia with olive oil and press with your fingertips all over the surface to create "dimples." Top with the onion, sliced potato, and Parmigiano-Reggiano. Sprinkle with sea salt.

Bake for 25 to 30 minutes, or until the edges are golden brown. Sprinkle with fresh sage and serve hot from the oven. *Serves 6 to 8*

PARMIGIANO, CORN, AND RED PEPPER MUFFINS

*Sweet corn and roasted red pepper make tasty muffins that are not
only good with salads and hot soups, but will enhance a brunch menu as well.*

1 cup all-purpose flour

1/2 cup (2 ounces) finely grated
   Parmigiano-Reggiano cheese

1/3 cup cornmeal

2 teaspoons baking powder

1/2 teaspoon baking soda

1/2 teaspoon salt

1 tablespoon sugar

2 scallions, minced (including 2 inches of the green tops)

1 red bell pepper, roasted, peeled, seeded, and chopped
   (see page 106)

1 cup fresh or frozen sweet corn kernels

3/4 cup sour cream

1/3 cup safflower oil

2 eggs

3 tablespoons coarsely grated Parmigiano-Reggiano cheese

Preheat the oven to 375°. Lightly oil a 12-cup muffin pan.

In a medium bowl, combine the flour, 1/2 cup finely grated Parmigiano-Reggiano, cornmeal, baking powder, baking soda, salt, and sugar. Mix well.

In a large bowl, combine the scallions, red pepper, corn, sour cream, oil, and eggs. Mix well.

Add the dry ingredients and stir just until moistened; do not overmix.

Spoon the batter into the muffin cups, filling them two-thirds full. Sprinkle with remaining Parmigiano-Reggiano. Bake for 18 to 20 minutes, or until golden brown. Transfer from the muffin pan to a wire rack. *Makes 1 dozen muffins*

SAUTÉED LEMON-GARLIC PRAWNS WITH PARMIGIANO-REGGIANO CREAM SAUCE

Seafood is usually not combined with Parmigiano-Reggiano in Italy. But this light sauce works well with the shrimp, and also with other meats and pasta.

16 prawns or jumbo shrimp, shelled and deveined
1/4 cup extra virgin olive oil
1/4 cup fresh lemon juice
1 teaspoon finely minced lemon zest
3 garlic cloves, minced
Salt and freshly ground pepper to taste
1 pound haricots verts or green beans, blanched

Parmigiano-Reggiano Cream Sauce
2 cups dry white wine
2 shallots, minced
2 cups chicken stock (see page 105)
1 cup heavy cream
2/3 cup (3 ounces) grated Parmigiano-Reggiano cheese
Salt and freshly ground white pepper to taste

Place the prawns in a shallow dish. Combine the olive oil, lemon juice, lemon zest, and garlic. Mix well and pour over the prawns. Marinate in the refrigerator for at least 1 hour, or up to overnight.

In a large sauté pan over medium heat, heat 2 tablespoons of the marinade. Using a slotted spoon, transfer the shrimp to the pan and sauté for 4 to 5 minutes, or until prawns are pink. Season with salt and pepper. Add the haricots verts and toss to heat. Turn out onto a warmed serving platter and serve with Parmigiano-Reggiano Cream Sauce on the side.

To make the sauce: In a large saucepan, combine the wine and shallots. Cook over high heat until most of the liquid has evaporated. Add the chicken stock and cook over high heat until reduced by half.

Add the cream and cook until hot. Stir in the Parmigiano-Reggiano. Season with salt and pepper.

Serves 4

Current Statistics

In 1996, the consortium's
650 registered Parmigiano-
Reggiano cheese producers
relied on 10,000 dairies
to create almost 3 million
cheeses. Of that, only
7 percent were exported
to other countries.

One ounce (28 grams)
of Parmigiano-Reggiano
provides 10 grams protein,
7 grams fat, 111 calories,
and 333 mg. of calcium.

THREE-CHEESE CALZONE

*If you don't have a pizza stone, just use a baking sheet lined
with parchment paper. Sprinkle it with a little cornmeal before placing the calzone
on it. My husband loves these stuffed with leftover risotto.*

1 package active dry yeast

2 tablespoons sugar

4 to 4^1/2 cups all-purpose flour

1 tablespoon salt

3 tablespoons extra virgin olive oil plus oil for brushing

1^1/2 cups warm water

^{3}/4 cup (3 ounces) grated skim milk mozzarella cheese

^{3}/4 cup (3 ounces) grated Parmigiano-Reggiano cheese

^{1}/2 cup (2^1/2 ounces) crumbled Gorgonzola cheese

Preheat the oven to 450° with a pizza stone inside.

Dissolve the yeast and sugar in ^{1}/2 cup of the warm water. Let stand for 5 minutes, or until foamy.

Put the flour and salt in a food processor fitted with the dough blade. Add the oil and process for 20 seconds. With the machine running, add the yeast mixture, then gradually add the remaining water in a steady stream until the mixture comes away from the sides of the workbowl. Process for 60 seconds longer.

On a lightly floured work surface, knead the dough into a ball. Put the dough in a lightly oiled bowl, cover and let rise in a warm place for 30 minutes.

Punch down the dough and divide it into 8 pieces. Form into balls; cover and let rise for 45 minutes.

Mix the cheeses together. Roll the dough into 6-inch circles. Brush with olive oil and top with cheese mixture. Fold in half, sealing the edges well. Brush with olive oil. Place on the pizza stone and bake for 10 minutes, or until golden brown.
Serves 8

Note: To make this dough by hand, mix together the flour and salt in a large bowl. Make a well in the center and add the yeast mixture and the remaining water. Work the liquid into the flour until you can no longer stir it. Turn it onto a lightly floured work surface and knead, adding flour as needed, until dough is smooth and not sticky, about 8 to 10 minutes.

Main dishes

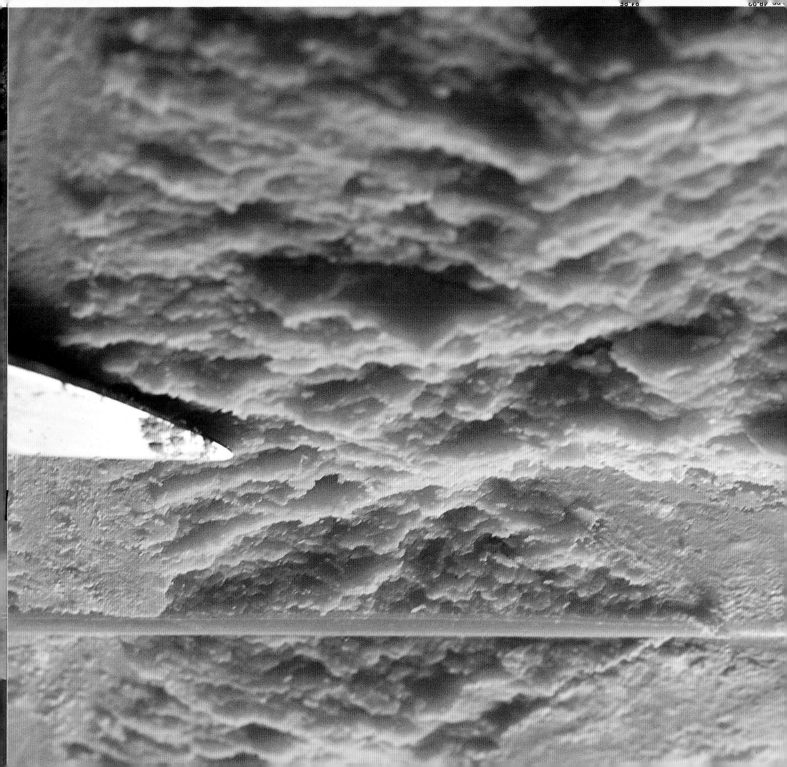

Finishes

PARMIGIANO-CRUSTED LEMON CHICKEN

This simple but delicious chicken recipe is great served on a bed of fettuccine with Parmigiano-Reggiano Cream Sauce (page 77). You can also substitute the lemon with orange. For a little extra flavor, add 1/2 teaspoon minced citrus zest to the sauce.

8 skinless, boneless chicken breast halves

Juice of 1 lemon

1 cup fresh bread crumbs

1/2 cup (2 ounces) finely grated Parmigiano-Reggiano cheese

1/2 cup walnuts, toasted and coarsely chopped (see page 106)

2 teaspoons finely grated lemon zest

1 tablespoon minced fresh flat-leaf parsley

1 teaspoon minced fresh thyme

1/2 teaspoon minced fresh rosemary

1/2 teaspoon minced fresh marjoram

1 teaspoon sea salt

1/2 teaspoon freshly ground pepper

2 large eggs beaten with 1 tablespoon milk

Flour for dredging

Preheat the oven to 375°. Lightly oil a 13 x 9-inch baking dish.

Place the chicken in a shallow dish and sprinkle both sides with lemon juice.

Spread the bread crumbs on a baking sheet and toast in the oven for 5 to 7 minutes, until golden brown. Let cool.

In a medium bowl, combine the Parmigiano-Reggiano, walnuts, lemon zest, parsley, thyme, rosemary, marjoram, salt and pepper. Add the toasted bread crumbs and mix well.

Dip each chicken breast into the beaten egg, dredge in the flour, dip in the egg again, and coat with the bread crumb mixture, pressing to coat well. Place in a single layer in the prepared baking dish and bake for 30 to 35 minutes, or until juices run clear when the breasts are pierced with a knife. Serve at once. *Serves 4*

CARAMELIZED PEARS WITH
PARMIGIANO-REGGIANO WEDGES

The classic combination of pears and Parmigiano-Reggiano makes a rich finish to a meal.
For a simpler version, omit the Grand Marnier and orange zest.

2 ripe but firm Bosc or Anjou pears, peeled, cored, and
  cut into 8 wedges
1/2 cup sugar
2 tablespoons unsalted butter
1/4 cup Grand Marnier
1 teaspoon finely grated orange zest
4 small Parmigiano-Reggiano wedges

Toss the pears and sugar together gently in a bowl.

In a large sauté pan over medium heat, melt the butter. Add the pears and cook over medium-high heat for 10 to 12 minutes, stirring occasionally, until sugar begins to caramelize to a light golden color. Do not let the sugar turn brown.

Add the Grand Marnier and orange zest. Cook 2 to 3 minutes longer, or until slightly reduced.

Transfer the mixture to serving dishes and serve immediately, with the Parmigiano-Reggiano on the side. *Serves 4*

Fragolini Parmigiani

There are several different grades of balsamic vinegar, from a low-quality commercial version to artisan quality. For this recipe, buy the best possible. At the minimum, it should be from Modena, Italy, and aged in wood barrels for at least 12 years. Artisan quality is very expensive, but you only need a few drops.

12 ounces fresh wild strawberries (or substitute domestic strawberries, sliced)

Aceto Balsamico Tradizionale, fine-quality balsamic vinegar

1 large wedge Parmigiano-Reggiano cheese

Freshly ground pepper (optional)

Serve small bowls of strawberries with the attendant condiments—Aceto Balsamico for drizzling, Parmigiano-Reggiano for chipping off individual shards, and a peppermill for those who want to try the tradition of grinding fresh pepper over the berries. *Serves 4*

BAKED APPLE CROWNS STUFFED
WITH HAZELNUT PRALINE

*The hazelnut praline recipe makes more than you'll need for this dish; store
the extra in an airtight container in a cool place until ready to use.*

Hazelnut Praline
3 1/4 cups (1 pound) hazelnuts, toasted and skinned
   (see page 106)
2 1/2 cups sugar
1/2 cup water

4 large Granny Smith or pippin apples
1/2 cup Hazelnut Praline, or granola
4 tablespoons butter, melted
8 small wedges Parmigiano-Reggiano cheese

To make the praline: Line a baking sheet with parchment paper.

In a heavy, medium saucepan, combine the sugar and water and boil until the mixture reaches 248°. Do not stir as it is heating. If crystals start to form on the sides of the pan, brush down with water on a pastry brush.

Add the nuts and remove from heat. Stir slowly until the sugar is grainy.

Return to heat and cook over medium heat until the sugar is a medium-dark caramel. Be careful not to burn it or yourself—it's very hot!

Pour onto the prepared baking sheet and let cool until hardened. Grind to a coarse texture by pulsing in a food processor. *Makes 3 cups*

To make the apple crowns: Preheat the oven to 375°. Line a medium baking dish with parchment paper.

Cut the unpeeled apples in half crosswise. Use a melon baller to scoop out the core, taking care not to cut all the way through the apple. With a paring knife, notch a zigzag edge around the top of each half, reserving the trimmings.

Chop the apple trimmings very fine and mix with the hazelnut praline and melted butter.

Spoon the mixture into the cavities, pressing to pack it in.

Place the apples on the prepared baking sheet and bake for 20 to 25 minutes, or until the apples are soft but not falling apart. Transfer to a wire rack to cool slightly before serving.

Spoon the pan juices over the apples and serve with wedges of Parmigiano-Reggiano. *Serves 8*

Basics

PASTA DOUGH

3 cups all-purpose flour
4 eggs
1 tablespoon safflower oil

Place the flour in a food processor fitted with the steel knife blade.

In a small container with a pour spout, whisk the eggs with the oil.

With processor running, slowly add the egg mixture until the dough starts to come away from the sides of the workbowl. Process for 30 seconds and check the consistency. The dough should be moist enough to pinch together, but not sticky.

On a lightly floured work surface, knead the dough to form a ball. Place in a plastic bag to rest.

Roll out one fourth of the dough at a time, keeping the remaining dough in the plastic bag to avoid drying it out.

Using a hand-cranked pasta maker, start on widest setting. Put the pasta through 8 to 10 times, folding it in half each time until the dough is smooth. If the dough tears, it may be too wet; dust it with flour, brushing off the excess.

Continue putting the dough through the rollers, without folding it, using a narrower setting each time until the dough is the desired thickness.

Allow the rolled dough to dry while rolling the next piece of dough, then cut into desired pasta shape. *Makes 1 pound*

Note: To make the dough by hand, place the flour on a work surface. Make a well in the center and put in the eggs and oil. With a fork, gradually blend the egg mixture into the flour. Knead by hand for 10 to 15 minutes, or until smooth and elastic.

CHICKEN STOCK

Stock freezes very well.
Try freezing it in 2- or 4-cup portions, to be
used later in soups or sauces.

One 3-pound chicken, cut up
1 carrot, peeled and cut into $1/2$-inch pieces
1 stalk celery, cut into $1/2$-inch pieces
1 onion, cut into $1/2$-inch pieces
Bouquet garni: 1 sprig parsley, 1 bay leaf,
   1 sprig thyme, 4 to 5 peppercorns
1 gallon water

Place all of the ingredients in nonaluminum stock pot and bring to a boil.

Reduce the heat to a simmer and skim the impurities from the top.

Simmer for 2 hours, skimming occasionally.

Strain and refrigerate the stock until the fat solidifies and can be removed. Makes 20 cups

Rich Chicken Stock: Simmer any amount of chicken stock until the volume is reduced by half.

ZESTY TOMATO SAUCE

Canned tomatoes work just fine in this recipe.
Use a 32-ounce can of whole tomatoes.
Drain and chop, reserving the packing liquid
to add back into your sauce.

3 tablespoons extra virgin olive oil
2 cloves garlic, minced
1 onion, finely chopped
10 ripe Roma tomatoes, peeled and coarsely chopped
   (see page 106)
$1/4$ cup minced fresh basil
$1/4$ cup minced fresh flat-leaf parsley
2 cups chicken stock (left)
1 teaspoon red pepper flakes, or to taste
Salt and freshly ground pepper to taste

In a large, heavy saucepan over medium heat, heat the oil and sauté the garlic and onion until soft, but not brown, about 3 minutes.

Add the tomatoes, basil, parsley, and chicken stock. Simmer until the sauce has reduced and thickened, about 30 to 45 minutes.

Purée half of the sauce in a blender and return to the pan. Season with pepper flakes, salt, and pepper. *Makes 8 cups*

Roasted Garlic

4 heads of garlic
1/2 cup olive oil
Salt and freshly ground pepper to taste

Preheat the oven to 300°.

Score around the middle of each head of garlic; do not cut into the cloves.Remove the top half of the papery skin, exposing the cloves.

Place the heads in a small oiled roasting pan and pour the olive oil over them. Season with salt and pepper, cover, and bake for 1 hour.

Uncover and bake 10 to 15 minutes longer, basting frequently, until heads are very tender. Let cool.

Pesto

4 cloves garlic, peeled
1 bunch fresh basil, stemmed
1/4 cup pine nuts, toasted (right)
1/2 cup extra virgin olive oil, or to desired consistency
1/4 cup (1 ounce) finely grated Parmigiano-Reggiano cheese

With a food processor running, drop in the garlic. Add the basil and pine nuts and process to a grainy texture. With the machine running, gradually add the olive oil to the desired consistency.

Roasting Peppers

Place whole peppers directly over a high flame. If you do not have a gas stovetop, use a grill or put the peppers on a baking sheet under your broiler. Turn the peppers frequently until blackened all over. Place them in a brown paper bag to steam and cool. Peel the peppers by scraping the blackened skin off with a sharp knife. Remove the stem and seeds before cutting as directed in the recipe.

Toasting Nuts

To toast walnuts and pine nuts, place on a dry baking sheet in a 350° oven for 6 to 10 minutes, until golden brown and aromatic.

To toast and skin hazelnuts, bake on a dry baking sheet at 325° for 10 to 12 minutes. Cool, then rub together in a kitchen towel until most of the brown skin has come off.

Peeling Tomatoes

Remove the core from each tomato. Drop in boiling water for 30 seconds; transfer immediately to ice water to stop the cooking and release the skins. The peel will slip off in your hands. To seed, cut the tomatoes in half crosswise and gently squeeze out the seeds.

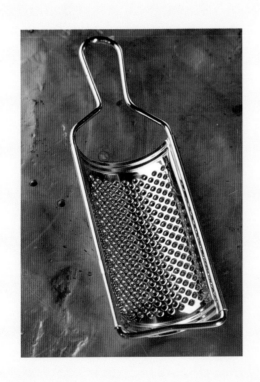

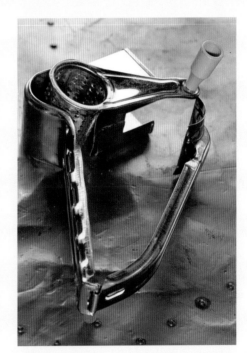

RESOURCES

Worth a Visit in Italy

Nothing is quite like tasting it in Italy. Just driving through the region will yield a wealth of serendipity. Watch for signs featuring a replica of a Parmigiano-Reggiano wheel along with a wedge of cheese. Signs with the word *vendita*, identify vendors who have cheese for sale. Many also sell fresh butter and ricotta cheese.

To telephone from the United States, dial 011-39 and the numbers listed below, omitting the first zero. When in Italy, dial the number as listed.

Consorzio del Formaggio Parmigiano-Reggiano

Via J. F. Kennedy, 18
Reggio Emilia
Tel. (0522) 77.741

Cheese Producer

Magnani Original Grana (founded in 1896)
Via I. Newton, 39a
Villa Gaida
Tel. (0522) 94.21.39

Giuseppe Magnani was the founder of the Consorzio del Formaggio Parmigiano-Reggiano. Coincidentally, this dairy, which is near Reggio Emilia, is managed today by the president of the consorzio, Paolo Delmonte. Magnani was a generous patron of the arts, and the Fondazione Magnani Rocca in Villa de Mamiano, near Parma, is a modern art museum with a good restaurant.

Cheese Shop

Otello dall'Asta
Via E. Copelli, 2e
Parma
Tel. (0521) 23.37.88

An excellent selection of Parmigiano-Reggiano, including *tenero*, the name for fresh Parmigiano that has not been aged.

Parmigiano-Reggiano Festival

On May 1, in Villa Aiola, a small village near Montecchio: A celebration of the famous cheese, with lots of food and a demonstration of the traditional process of making the cheese over a wood fire in an eighteenth-century *caseificio* (cheese-producing facility).

Restaurants

Osteria di Rubbiara
Via Risaia, 2
Nonantola
Tel. (059) 54.90.19

This little restaurant near Modena is owned by Italo Pedroni, a producer of balsamic vinegar. The classic dishes prepared by his wife are moderately priced. You can count on a piece of Parmigiano-Reggiano drizzled with Pedroni's aged balsamic vinegar. Go very hungry because Italo likes his customers to clean their plates. Reservations are strongly suggested.

Ristorante Parizzi
Via Repubblica, 71
Parma
Tel. (0521) 28.59.52

Ristorante Parizzi is one of the *Buon Ricordo* restaurants. All over Italy, a few special restaurants have been selected by this organization to commemorate their house specialty with a souvenir plate. The plate has the name of the restaurant and a rustic drawing of the special dish; if you order that item, you can bring the plate home with you. The *Buon Ricordo* specialty here is *Tortelli d'erbetta alla parmigiana* (herbed tortelli pasta).

Mail-Order Sources

Di Palo Fine Foods
206 Grand Street
New York, NY 10013
Tel. (212) 226-1033
There are suppliers and there are suppliers. Louis Di Palo has some of the best choices of Parmigiano-Reggiano and offers some of the most resourceful advice. Hand-selected Parmigiano-Reggiano available at peak seasonality; you can also request cheese by area, mountain or plains.

Williams-Sonoma, stores nationwide
Catalogue Tel. (800) 541-2233
Vacuum-packed Parmigiano-Reggiano; hard cheese knife.

Dean and Deluca
560 Broadway
New York, NY
Tel. (212) 226-6800
Catalogue Tel. (800) 221-7714
Parmigiano-Reggiano; *segna forme* (used for scoring the rind of hard cheeses) or the almond-shaped *grana* knife.

Balducci
424 Sixth Avenue
New York, NY
Tel. (212) 673-2600
Catalogue Tel. (800) 225-3822
Parmigiano-Reggiano.

Manicaretti
5332 College Avenue, No. 200
Oakland, CA 94618
Tel. (800) 799-9830
Artisan quality farro, pasta, risotto, and capers.

For Further Reference

Anderson, Burton. *Treasures of the Italian Table*, New York: William Morrow, 1994.

Bonilauri, Franco *Parmigiano Reggiano: A Symbol of Culture and Civilization*, Reggio Emilia: Leonardo Arte, 1993.

Bugialli, Giuliano. *Classic Techniques of Italian Cooking*, New York: Simon & Schuster, 1982.

Consorzio del Formaggio Parmigiano-Reggiano, Via J. F. Kennedy, 18, 42100 Reggio Emilia, Italy. Tel. (39) 522.77.741 Information available on the Internet at http://www.parmigiano-reggiano.it:80/

Field, Carol. *Celebrating Italy*, New York: William Morrow, 1990.

Kasper, Lynne Rossetto. *The Splendid Table: Recipes from Emilia-Romagna, the Heartland of Northern Italian Food*, New York: William Morrow, 1992.

Slow Food, Via Mendicità Istruita, 14, 12042 Bra (CN), Italy. Tel. (39) 172.41.12.73; Fax (39) 172.42.12.93.

General Index

Recipe Index

ACKNOWLEDGMENTS

Pamela Sheldon Johns would like to thank the following people:

My husband, Courtney Johns, for his patient support and excellent reading and tasting skills.

Jennifer Barry for conceiving the idea for this book, for being so great to work with, and for creating, along with Kristen Wurz, a beautiful book.

Philippa Farrar for her thoughtful and precise testing of the recipes, and all of the home recipe testers for their valuable comments: Mary Bartolli, Elizabethe Branstetter, Judy Dawson, Kate Dole and Bruce McGuire, Debbie Duggan, Nancy Edney, Michelle Fingert, Marilyn Greenberg, Linda Hale, Diana Harris, Kelley Johnson, Paula L. Knight, Marilyn Makepeace, Tim Neenan, Stan Nicolaides, Donna Pinckney, Laurence Pinnolis, Monica Salcedo, Amy Sloan, Glenda Spoonemore, Joyce Trevillian, and Joan Willicombe.

Mary Abbott Hess for assistance with nutritional details.

And thanks to my friends and family who offered support in many ways: Anne Dickerson, Michelle Fingert, Keri Jo Johns, Julia Loya, Juliana Middleton, Janice Ross, and Edna Sheldon.

Jennifer Barry Design would like to acknowledge the following individuals and establishments for their help and support on this book project:

Special thanks to Kirsty Melville, publisher of Ten Speed Press, for her enthusiam for our project, and to Lorena Jones, senior production editor, for her editorial help and guidance.

Nancy Radke and Martha Williams of Ciao Limited for their assistance on our project and photography planning abroad and at home. Leo Bertozzi of the Consorzio del Formaggio Parmigiano-Reggiano for his kind assistance in Italy, as guide and liason for the visits to the Parmigiano *casello*.

Maria Hjelm for her kind support and her marketing expertise, Jenny Collins for proofreading, Anne Dickerson for her editorial advice, and special thanks to Vicki Kalish of Williams-Sonoma for her advice and support.

The photography team would like to thank Biordi Italian Imports, San Francisco; Frank Mancuso of Vivande/PortaVia, San Francisco; Bruno Quercini and Amy Edelen of Pane e Vino Trattoria, San Francisco; Niebaum-Coppola Estate Winery, Rutherford; Leonard's 2001 and Judy Goldsmith Antiques, San Francisco; and Barbara Chambers.